Five in a Row

Volume Three

Inspired learning through great books.

Ages 5-9

Second Edition

By Jane Claire Lambert

Five in a Row Volume Three

Second Edition

ISBN 978-1-888659-24-5

Content contributions by Carrie Bozeman and Rebekah Matt
Layout and cover design by Michael Bozeman

Published by:
Five in a Row Publishing
312 SW Greenwich Dr.
Suite 220
Lee's Summit, MO 64082
816-866-8500

Send all requests for information to the above address.

For
Our Michigan "five"-
Sarah, Alex, Jacob, Kevan and Lucas

and

Martha C.

Contents

Introduction

Good books have always been the doorway to learning. That doorway leads to growth and an appreciation for the wonders around us. Come along on a learning adventure using picture books to open the door to art, history, vocabulary, geography, science, human relationships, applied math and writing!

No matter how young, children get a substantial educational head start from books. *Five in a Row* has been created to bring excitement and fun to learning and to enrich children's lives through wonderful children's literature. These lesson plans are simple in concept, but rich in results. Read the chosen book in its entirety each day for at least a week. After each reading, choose an exercise to share with your student, and watch their world expand as you begin to show them facets of the story they would never have recognized without your purposeful guidance. As a teacher of this material, you will find that you become excited and interested in a variety of subjects too. You'll rediscover the joy of learning and you'll build a special bond between you and your student as the two of you go on a learning adventure together.

This curriculum is intended to be extremely flexible, allowing you the option to do any or all of the exercises for each story. You may elect to skip over certain lessons which do not fit the needs of your student and you may place additional emphasis on certain ones which seem appropriate. You will find more exercises than you can use in a week, so enjoy choosing just the right lesson elements for your students.

You can adjust classroom time to fit your needs as well. By using only one lesson element each day, you can work through *Five in a Row* in as little as 30 minutes daily, including the time to read the book. If you choose to use all of the lesson elements, field trips and follow-up exercises, you could easily spend several hours daily. Use *Five in a Row* however it best suits your needs and the needs of your students.

The technique of reading the same story for at least five days in a row is one that I have tested in teaching for many years. I continue to be amazed at the effectiveness of this technique! Each book will become very special to the children. They will remember more and more about the story, but more importantly, they will begin to think more critically (even five year olds!) as they begin wondering how certain portions of the story came to be, or how the characters solved a certain problem. These results could never be achieved in just one reading. (See page 10 for the complete teaching theory behind the concept of *Five in a Row*.)

Students will see how the illustrator accomplished certain effects and they'll be encouraged to begin exploring those techniques in their own art. You'll see your students learning about science, history and applied math through everyday discussions. Your students will have the opportunity to try new activities they read about, or to learn more about a variety of people, places or animals. You'll also discover your student asking more questions than ever before. By the end of the week, a new book will have become their friend for life.

Perhaps the most valuable benefit of using *Five in a Row* is that young students learn to fully evaluate a work (with your guidance), and that skill will serve them well as they learn to read for themselves. Your students will begin looking to see whether a book is a Caldecott or a Newbery medal winner. They'll quickly classify a new book as either fact or fiction. They'll be able to articulate the point of view from which the story has been written. They will know about a wide variety of literary techniques and learn to recognize them for themselves. You'll be delighted when your students begin to evaluate the illustrator's medium and technique.

All of this is imparted in an enjoyable learning environment. Students think you're just reading them a book, but they're learning so much every day! The more lessons you do together, the more skills your young students will acquire; skills which will benefit them through high school, college and throughout life!

Welcome to the wonderful world (and the second edition!) of *Five in a Row*. Even though our world has changed greatly since the first edition, the purpose and mission of this highly effective curriculum remain the same: to provide students with a quality educational foundation for their elementary years with "inspired learning through great books." This second edition is up to date regarding today's technology while continuing to base learning on high-quality, carefully chosen books and lessons—including all-new activity sheets following each title. You are the leader for this adventure, so gather the children around you and have a great time!

Jane Claire Lambert
May 1994; June 2020

About the Books Themselves

*"The goal of our instruction is to lead children to fall in love
with good books and and to embrace the joy of learning."*

Sutherland and Arbuthnot write in the classic children's literature textbook *Children and Books*, "Aesthetic satisfaction comes to small children as well as to adults, and the development of their taste depends not only on their initial capacities but also on *the material they encounter and the way in which it is presented*."* (emphasis added)

If you're like most of us, you can directly attribute a lifelong interest in at least one topic to the quality and creativity with which some particular teacher or a parent introduced the subject to you as a child. Likewise, you may well have nurtured a lifelong distaste for certain subjects for the same reason: an unpleasant early experience.

Sutherland and Arbuthnot go on to suggest that by selecting excellent children's literature and reading it together each day, children have the opportunity to "catch a new theme, savor the beauty, the subtle humor or a special meaning that eluded them at first."

"Sometimes," the authors continue, "an adult has the privilege of seeing this discovery take place. The children's faces come suddenly alive; their eyes shine. They may be anticipating an amusing conclusion or a heroic triumph. There is a sudden chuckle or breath is exhaled like a sigh. The book has moved them, perhaps even to laughter or tears; in any case there is a deep inner satisfaction and they will turn to books again with anticipation."

Sutherland and Arbuthnot conclude, "Once they have experienced the joy of reading they have acquired a habit that will serve them all their lives. It is important, therefore, that those who guide their reading select wisely."

It is within this context that the titles for *Five in a Row* have been chosen. In each case, content was of supreme importance. Books were chosen that showcase close family relationships, personal triumphs, and persevering in times of trial. There are books with people characters and stories with animal characters, but in all the stories the characters touch the reader's heart and demonstrate life's truths. Please remember, however, that our selection of a particular title by an author does *not* mean that we necessarily endorse *everything* from that author. We're aware of several cases where authors have written marvelous books and very questionable books as well. Please take the time to review any book you bring home from the library *before* reading it to your children!

In addition to content, the books also cover a wide range of artistic expression: from the realistic paintings of Ted Rand to the whimsical pictures of Patricia Polacco; from the chalk pastels of Thomas B. Allen to the bright, colorful illustrations of Karen Barbour. Each title was selected for a diversity of magnificent art, beautifully rendered for the utter appreciation and enjoyment of children. Art to appreciate, art to learn from and art to be remembered for a lifetime!

It has been said some stories must be talked over or listened to while *someone who knows and loves them reads aloud*. If *you* come to love the stories, your student will too.

With these standards in mind, we hope you and your student find a special place in your heart for these stories and for the concept of *Five in a Row*.

*Sutherland and Arbuthnot, *Children and Books*, Harper Collins Publishers, 8th ed., 1991.

How to Use Five in a Row

Select a book to study with your student. There is no right or wrong order for covering the material; it's entirely up to you the order that you choose. Please also note that the books in Volumes 1-3 are interchangeable in difficulty; the books do not get "harder" as you move through these three volumes. (Volume 4, however, increases in complexity and depth and is ideal for older elementary-aged students.)

Some teachers will choose to purchase each book as a valuable addition to their permanent library. Of course, most public libraries should have (or be able to request) each of the titles in this book. (See "Finding the Books" at the end of this manual for more information.)

Important Note: Please take the time to read the book aloud to your student each day before covering the lesson material. *Five in a Row* was designed and tested to be read daily! The repetition is essential to your student's learning process, and the time you spend reading together is just as important as the lesson material itself. For more information on *why* to read the story five days in a row, and suggestions if you have a child who resists this idea, see "Reading the Stories Five Days in a Row" on page 25.

Following the story units in this manual, you will find a sample planning worksheet for *The Duchess Bakes a Cake*. You'll also find a blank worksheet which you can reproduce and use for each FIAR story that you study. The sample sheet shows how to correlate the teacher's guide suggestions and plans to the five days of the week you will study each particular book. Or, feel free to design your own worksheet. Some teachers don't care to use planning sheets at all, and just work directly from the *Five in a Row* manual. Do whatever works for you!

Notice that the sample lesson plan is outlined briefly and gives you a quick reference for the week. Not every lesson suggested in the manual under *The Duchess Bakes a Cake* is listed on the sample lesson—there are too many lessons for one week. So you will choose the ones that are especially suited to your student and list them on the blank planning sheet. While the subjects Math, Science, Art, etc., do not have to be used in the same order every week, remember that when planning a class week, the curriculum builds on itself. Whatever you study on

Monday will be recognized by your student when you read the story again on Tuesday. When you read the story a third time on Wednesday, the lessons you introduced on Monday and Tuesday will not escape the student's notice as he hears or sees the examples again. So each lesson, except the one for Friday, gets at least one review and some lessons get four reviews. The topics you think are most important, therefore, should be scheduled toward the beginning of the week. It seems as though Art often gets tagged in the Friday slot. Try using this topic earlier in the week, perhaps on Wednesday, so your student can study the pictures for several days as he hears the story read and reread.

Also following the story units, you will find a sheet of story disks. These are quick, symbolic representations of the sixteen titles included in *Five in a Row*. They are meant to be used in conjunction with a laminated world or U.S. map. First, color the disk and put the name of the book on the back of the disk. For greater durability, laminate the disks before you cut them apart (or use clear contact paper after cutting). By placing a Velcro® dot on the disk and the other dot on the map where it goes, you can quickly take it off and put it back on each day (tacky putty will also work). Eventually you will be able to track the stories you have read all over the world. Even young students will learn some map basics. Any stories with fictitious settings can be placed in the margins of the map as the "Land of Make Believe."

There is also a page of blank disks so you can make your own pictures for these stories, or replace a lost disk. You might also like to make disks for other stories you read outside of *Five in a Row*.

Social Studies

Because there are only five subject categories (to correspond to the five days of the week), many different topics are included under Social Studies. Each story has a specific geographic area, and often the culture of that area is discussed. Making a flag is fun and informative, and you'll find flags to color in many units, as well as a "Parts of a Flag" reference sheet at the end of this manual. Geography also includes the mention of oceans, continents and geographic regions. (An excellent illustrated children's geography book is Rand McNally's *Picture Atlas of the World*, illustrated by Brian Delf. You'll find it informative and fun!) Under the topic Social Studies, you will also find lessons about character traits, disappointments, perseverance, different cultures, occupations and much more. In addition, the Social Studies unit includes history. Under this heading, you will see lessons which create opportunities to discuss the American Revolution and the Civil War, the Gold Rush, medieval times, pioneers and settlers, mountain culture, and more. Social Studies also includes several lessons about people and their relationships to one another. As you can see, a wide variety of subjects is included under Social Studies.

Choose the topics you'd like to discuss and either mark them in the manual or write them on the Planning Sheet under whichever day it seems best to cover them. If you use the Planning Sheets, be sure when presenting the material to tie it in to the story.

Language Arts

There are many techniques for learning Language Arts using children's literature. Increasing vocabulary, learning literary devices, learning list-making skills, composing short stories and acting out dramas are just a few of the ways. Teaching Language Arts is a natural extension of the enjoyment of children's literature.

Vocabulary is enriched by hearing new words like pelter (*Amber on the Mountain*), junction (*The Bee Tree*) or stealthy (*Paul Revere's Ride*). A child's vocabulary is much greater than just the words he can read or spell, and reading a story which contains new words five times in a row will help increase his recognition and understanding of those words.

windmill

a machine that uses wind power to grind grain, pump water and make electricity

pink

color swatch

a tint of the color red, made by mixing red and white paint

Two methods for organizing vocabulary words are the file box and the notebook. The file box method uses four-by-six inch, unlined index cards with alphabet dividers. Either the teacher or the student can print the word at the top left of the card. Write in a short definition at the left, and either draw an illustration or or print a picture to show the word visually. Keep the words alphabetized and encourage your student to go through the cards frequently. This will help him remember which story each word was from. (To help in remembering the source, write the name of the book on the back of the card.)

A second method of keeping track of vocabulary words is to list them on a page in the Language Arts or Vocabulary section of a notebook. Print the word (large, if necessary) and illustrate with a drawing or picture as a visual reminder. Lists can be alphabetized or organized by FIAR title. Review these words from time to time while remembering your favorite incidents in the corresponding stories.

A notebook is good for more than just vocabulary words. In fact, it's a great way for a student to keep his work organized and ready for quick review and easy reference. For the grade-level student, this will likely come naturally. But for the very young student, to have his own notebook is special. For him, use colored dividers so he can find the subjects, even if he cannot yet read. In this way, he can proudly find his Science section and show someone his drawings or projects. He'll be able to look up his Vocabulary section with illustrations and share his art work with others.

List-making is another Language Arts skill that develops vocabulary, memory, associations and creativity. It is also a skill that has lifetime value in many different areas, from grocery lists, lists of people to invite to a party, "to do" lists, lists of ways to solve a problem, to descriptive lists that inform. There have been great, eloquent lists made by famous people of the things they liked, disliked, or the things they wished for. Once, while travelling together in a car, a friend's family began an oral list of methods of transportation. Many miles down the road, the list had grown to gigantic proportions with the hilarious inclusions of walking on stilts and walking on your hands added to the regular methods of riding in a car, bus or taxi. What began as a list-making exercise became entertainment. The art and skill of good list-making is included in this curriculum to provide both a learning experience and a good time.

There are many **literary devices** explained in FIAR and tied in to the lessons from children's literature. You probably will not cover them all, but they are included to remind the teacher of them and give opportunities for casual inclusion in the reading lessons.

As you come to each new literary device, a list can be made with examples and pictures. Keep your list in the Language Arts section of the student's notebook. For instance, personification (giving human qualities to non-human things) might be defined and illustrated with a picture of the Pillsbury Doughboy® or Lightning McQueen from the movie *Cars*. Other literary devices can be illustrated, as well. Keeping a chart or list of these words makes review easy and interesting and can be used by the student as an inspirational list when he is creating his own works.

Ideas for leading your student into writing include letting them record their stories, which you then transcribe. Often the student will enjoy listening to his story in his own voice. Writing rebus stories, where pictures take the place of certain words throughout the story, is an interesting way to begin writing skills. As you follow the curriculum, you'll find lessons in what makes a good story, and ways to achieve variety. Your student will begin to appreciate the choices an author makes to create a story and the careful thought that goes into writing.

Many times in this curriculum these type of questions are asked: "How does the author make the story exciting? What words does he use? How does he...?" Eventually, as he sees these techniques modeled before him, the student will begin to include such elements in his own writing. The suggestion after every lesson to imitate an aspect of the author's work is optional, depending on the interest and abilities of the student. See if your student enjoys imitating the author's techniques. If not, just concentrate on appreciating the lesson. In time the rest will follow.

If, however, your student enjoys writing "after the manner of," imitating aspects of the author's story, he will like the suggestions to try a fable, an instructional story or a poem. He'll also begin to include a good setting, interesting characters, an exciting climax, or an important denouement (final outcome) in his own stories. Each of these is a separate lesson in the curriculum. Again, keeping a chart or a good notebook list filled with definitions and examples will give your student a ready reference when he is writing his own stories and makes review easy. Just add to the list or chart on an ongoing basis as you come to different lessons (see the Choices a Writer Can Make activity sheet at the end of the manual).

Remember, there are too many language arts topics to be covered in a single day. Choose the ones appropriate for your student and jot them briefly on the planning sheet under the day you think best. Also remember, if you are going to teach vocabulary it is a good idea to do this at the beginning of the week, perhaps on Tuesday. As the book is read and reread throughout the week, your student will see familiar vocabulary words again and again, providing a built-in review. Depending on your child's age, you may want to choose only a few words from each story.

Art

When you choose good children's literature, you will frequently discover exceptional illustrations, as well. Watercolor, pastels, charcoal, beautiful colors, active lines, funny characters and balanced compositions are all parts of fine illustrations for children. Furthermore, they can be used to introduce even young children to fundamentals and techniques of art.

Appreciating art is learning to recognize the many techniques and concepts which combine to produce effective art while learning what you like and why. Some pictures have a rhythm, balance and choice of color that combine to make them pleasing. Some illustrations are meant to evoke strong emotions or to provide information. Even young children can begin to identify great art wherever it's encountered. They'll also begin to know why they like it. By teaching about the artist and their methods, your student's taste in art will expand to include a rich and wonderful variety of work.

As you look at illustrations with your student, ask, "What do you think the illustrator used for his medium?" Sometimes it's hard to tell (check the copyright page of the book, which sometimes will provide this information). There are combinations of pen and ink with watercolor washes, etchings with strokes from oil or acrylic and the wet, transparent blends of watercolors. Look for the shading in a charcoal or pencil sketch, or the buildup of color by successive layers of colored pencils. Learn to identify the deep texture of pastels.

After you've discussed the medium, ask "why and how" questions. "Why do you think the illustrator chose this medium, color, style, viewpoint, etc.? How did the artist make it look like nighttime, etc.?" These kinds of questions will open a doorway to art appreciation for your student.

Let him study the illustrations as he tries to answer your questions. You may want to suggest some answers as you discuss the methods the artist used and how the illustrations help tell the book's story. Does the artist's work provide additional story information not included in the text? Does the choice of color palette convey the tone of the story?

Asking lots of questions will cause your student to look with a more critical eye. He will pore over the pages to find answers and he will gain a love of art based on newly-discovered information. This will lead to an emerging appreciation for great illustrations. Don't ask all the questions at the same time. Bring them up conversationally from time to time as you study each book.

One of the best techniques for teaching art fundamentals is to imitate a particular technique from the painting or drawing of a known artist. In *Five in a Row*, the lessons attempt to identify and single out a specific artistic element and to encourage imitation. Your student will be invited to mimic specific styles, colors and designs. Remember that appreciation usually precedes imitation. Therefore, look for examples of the element you are studying in other books or online. Let him examine and enjoy these additional examples before he begins experimenting with the technique himself.

In order for you to be ready to meet your student's needs, you may want to have certain supplies on hand:

Kneadable eraser

Drawing pencil or #2 lead pencil

Charcoal - (**Teacher's Note:** Supervise the use of charcoal, since it can get messy!)

Oil Pastels - The favorite medium of many young students. They don't smear as much as chalky pastels. (**Adult supervision required**.)

Markers

Colored pencils - Look for good colored pencils. They make a difference.

Crayons - Look for "name brand" crayons.

Watercolors - Prang® brand is good, or tube watercolors are extremely easy to use for mixing exercises.

Acrylics - Not necessary, but it gives your student a chance to paint layer upon layer using lighter colors on top.

Brushes - You'll need brushes with several different bristle lengths and widths. If you want to paint fine-lined tree branches, you'll need the right brush!

Watercolor paper

Canvas paper for acrylics

Drawing tablet or paper

Tracing paper

Ruler

Templates of various geometric shapes cut from cardboard or cardstock

Above all, remember that creative art is an intensely personal subject. If you wish to demonstrate a technique, do it on a separate piece of paper—never on your student's own work! Be wise with your criticism of his progress. Grant him the respect you would grant any artist. Go slowly, letting him catch the enthusiasm for the ideas you present.

Math

In many of the books chosen for this curriculum, children will enjoy finding practical ways to use the new concepts they learn in math.

For the youngest student, there are many opportunities for counting practice. It may be counting the stars in one illustration or fence pickets in another. Finding and counting all the pizza toppings in *Little Nino's Pizzeria* is fun! It will also provide a time for the teacher to see and hear the student count actual objects.

Measuring liquid and dry ingredients are covered in the lessons for *The Duchess Bakes a Cake*. You may also introduce tallying in *Henry the Castaway* and counting by tens in *The Wild Horses of Sweetbriar*.

The concepts of relative size, measuring, time, and money are all found in the stories of children's picture books. A book about quilts offers a chance to talk about geometric shapes. Because the concepts are linked to an enjoyable story, your student will remember them with pleasure.

If time is available, especially in the summer before school starts, make math manipulatives using ideas from the story illustrations. For instance, if you are going to read a book for a week that is about trains, make flash cards with the facts printed inside train cars. Use bright, cheerful colors and write the answers on the back. Laminating the cards will help them last. The cards can also contain any term or new concept on one side with the definition on the other.

$2 + 8 =$

Front

10

Back

$7 - 4 = 3$

Front

difference

Back

Reading the story all the way through while enjoying the closeness of the teacher and the entertainment of the book establishes a good environment for presenting a math lesson derived from the story. Even the lesson will be a shared experience. If there are more math ideas than are appropriate for one day, choose the ones you wish to cover and write them on the planning sheet for the day you wish to cover Math.

Science

Open wide the door to children's literature and find within the stories a vast array of scientific educational potential: from gazing at the stars and wondering about our moon, to thinking about equinox and solstice, flora and fauna, metamorphosis and life cycles, seasons, nutrition, animal behavior and much more.

After reading the book for the day, bring up conversationally the science topics suggested in the lessons and other ideas that you may have. Don't try to use all the topics. *The Salamander Room,* for instance, includes science topics of love of nature, scavenger hunt, salamanders, crickets, butterflies, and animal classification. Just choose the ones you think are appropriate and mark them on the planning sheet on whichever day seems best.

When presenting your science lesson, *be sure to tie it into the story.* For instance, in *Henry the Castaway,* you might say, turning to the first page, "Remember when Henry was on the river? What kinds of things might you find near a river?"

A science section in your student's notebook with a page for Ocean Life, a page for Simple Machines, etc., will help in reviewing lessons he's studied. If he likes, let your student illustrate the topics with his own drawings of the story. This could be part of a beloved notebook by year's end.

Note: *Five in a Row* was created to be gender-neutral and you'll find a wide variety of fascinating lessons that appeal to both boys and girls. Don't assume that a boy may not enjoy a story that has a girl as the main character, or vice versa! And, please note that we've referred to "teacher and student" in the singular. Many of you will have more than one student. Another item of note is that throughout the lessons, some words have been defined within parentheses. This is done to remind teachers of very young students that even *seemingly common* terms may have to be explained!

If you are new to *Five in a Row*, here are some valuable thoughts from Jane Claire to help you get the most out of your experience.

There are two sections included here. One is a conversational scripted week using some of the lessons from the *Five in a Row* manual. It will give you an idea of what a week could look like. The second is an explanation of how and why the curriculum was developed, including the educational philosophy and many tips for overcoming opposition to multiple story readings should you happen to have a reluctant student.

A Conversational Presentation of a Five in a Row Unit

There is of course no "absolute" way to present *Five in a Row* lessons. Each family modifies their presentation to fit a wide variety of needs. However, let me explain an effective way to use this curriculum using *The Story About Ping* (from FIAR Volume 1) for our example. There are usually several lessons for each subject category listed in your *Five in a Row* manual. In this demonstration I will not use every lesson listed but will select certain ones to illustrate the conversational teaching technique.

Whatever time in the day you choose to do your *Five in a Row* lessons, begin by cuddling up on the sofa or big chair and saying: "Let's read a book together!" Then enjoy reading a good story all the way through.

Day One

On the first day, after you've read the story through together, you simply begin conversationally, "Did you notice that our story today takes place in a foreign country? Do you remember the name of the country?" Or you could ask, "Where was it that Ping lived?" If your child doesn't remember, look in the story and find a line where it says that Ping lived in China.

Ask your student if he knows where China is. If he does, then let him show you on a world map. If he doesn't, then help him find China and the Yangtze River on a world map. The story disk (included at the end of each FIAR manual) is a wonderful manipulative which your student can use to pinpoint the setting of the story and enjoy reviewing it, on the map, each of the five days that you cover *The Story About Ping*.

Now continue by asking your student if he has ever heard of people living on boats like the one in the story? Can he see the door and windows in the illustration of the wise-eyed boat? Some of the people of China live on their boats and fish for their dinner and eat whatever they catch. Ask your student if he would like to live on a boat and never know what he was going to have for dinner till he went fishing each day. (Now, there are no right or wrong answers for this type of question. Some children will respond to this line of questioning with, "Cool! I'd love to live on a boat and fish for my dinner!" while others will say, "No way! Take me to McDonald's!" This is one of the wonderful ways that *Five in a Row* works. This curriculum helps you get to *really know* your child. And as you share with him, he will get to know you better, as well!)

Continue talking about the length of the Yangtze River and how the people of China live, using the facts listed in your manual. Please note that you do not have to use all of the information on China if you have a younger child. For some five-year-olds, for instance, just learning that there is a place called China and that it is far away is a great start!

Proceed with as much information from the lessons as you think would be interesting and enjoyable for the student you are teaching. Though the information in your manual is certainly enough, it is still fun to find a simple book or two on China at your library. The pictures are colorful and interesting. You could also search for pictures of China online.

There are many ideas in the "How to Use *Five in a Row*" section of your manual on how to help your student document what he has learned through making pages for his notebook, creating card files, or using the activity pages provided at the end of each unit. You can also visit www.fiveinarow.com for Fold & Learns for several of the books in *Before Five in a Row*, *Five in a Row*, and *Beyond Five in a Row*, Note-booking Pages for use with all ages, and other helpful products.
This completes your first day of Five in a Row.

Day Two

The next day you would say (with enthusiasm!), "We're going to read *The Story About Ping* again." For most students this is exactly what they want to do! If your child is hesitant, just say, "Today we're going to read the story and we will be learning how a story is written! Marjorie Flack who wrote *The Story About Ping* has done something special with the words and we're going to see if we can hear what she has done." Then you read the story again. (Your student is listening, but he will also be thinking,

Oh, Ping lives in China," and "no I wouldn't like to live on one of those boats and wow, the Yangtze river sure is long—it's longer than a trip to my grandpa's." All the things you talked about the day before will be running through his head. Reading the story again makes review easy, doesn't it?

On day two, you can ask your student if he can put the story disk on China. (You can vary the question each day: Where did Ping live? What was the name of the country where our story takes place? What was the name of the long river in China? Can you find it?

Since you have just reread the story it is time to share how the author used a special sentence several times in the story. Read the sentence and ask your student if he can remember where else that sentence was used in the book? If he can't, just find the places in the story where the sentence is repeated and show your student how the author uses the same words in the middle of the story and again at the end. Explain that authors sometimes use an interesting sentence several times in a story to make it fun...we call that *repetition* (like repeating). An author wouldn't want to use repetition too much, but a little repetition can make a story interesting.

Ask your student if he would like to write a short story (or you can work on it together) using an interesting sentence at the beginning of the paragraph and again at the end? This story can be very simple. The idea is to give your student a chance to try using repetition as the author in *The Story About Ping* did.

If you are keeping a running chart of "Choices a Writer Can Make," (provided at the end of this manual) list repetition as one of those choices. You can add to this list each time you have a lesson on literary techniques and your list provides an easy way to review! Later, when your student wants to write a story of his own, he can go over the list and be reminded of the special ways that great authors have created stories that are interesting and enjoyable. You will see him begin to use some of these techniques in his writings, too.

Your student's writings can be illustrated and placed in the Language Arts section of his notebook. If he is too young to write, you may take his ideas or stories in dictation and let him illustrate his work and place it in his notebook under Language Arts.

Remember that *Five in a Row* does not teach "how to read." You may enjoy looking into *Reading Made Easy* for that portion of your teaching day.

You may stop here or go on to do another lesson from the Language Arts section. *This is the end of day two with Five in a Row.*

Day Three

On day three you'll reread the story again, this time promising some interesting art lessons to follow. (The art lessons have been placed on Wednesday so that there will be two more days of reading the book and looking at the pictures.) Today as you read the story your child will be thinking, "China… boat…oh, there's that repetitious sentence we talked about yesterday!"

After reading the story, you'll mention that Kurt Wiese was the artist who created the illustrations for *The Story About Ping*. It looks as though he may have used some colored pencils. "Let's pick a few of the pictures to look at and see how many colors he used. Do the colors look like they blend together? Why don't we use some colored pencils and paper and see how yellow over red looks and maybe some yellow over blue."

Continue with some of the other art lessons. They are easy to explain and quick to do. Again, you may want to keep a running list of "Choices an Artist Can Make" (also provided at the end of this manual) and include, as you go through the year, different mediums and other techniques. This list will serve as a point for review and allow your student to choose techniques from the list that he wants to include in his own art project of the moment.

Any art work done can be placed in the student's notebook under Art, along with illustrated examples of art techniques discussed from the book's illustrator. *This completes day three of Five in a Row.*

Day Four

For Thursday, the reading of the story will have your student thinking of and recognizing all the previous lessons including a whole new look at the illustrations. Don't forget to find China on the map with the story disk. (Take the disk down each day before the lesson, so that your student can replace it on the map. Always help him cheerfully if needed.)

Proceed to the Applied Math lesson. These lessons are usually developed from the story to show children how math is used in their everyday world. *The Story About Ping* has only one math lesson and it is a counting one. It can be skipped by the older *Five in a Row* users and you can substitute additional lessons from other topic sections, if you wish. In this counting lesson the ducks can be counted, counted by two's, grouped, etc. Most of the story units will have multiple lessons for Applied Math. Remember that when your student is ready to begin a math curriculum, you need to find one even though you are doing the Applied Math lessons from *Five in a Row*. These Applied Math lessons are *not* a substitute for a regular math curriculum; they instead serve as an introduction and inspiration for ideas about math. ***This completes day four of Five in a Row.***

Day Five

On Friday, you will read the story for the last time. Imagine all the things your student is remembering as you read together! Most of the time when children read a book, they only think about the plot. Through using *Five in a Row*, they learn that a book has so much more to offer! There is often geography, history, foreign culture, character lessons, interesting ways that language is used and techniques by which great stories are written, amazing art, sometimes math, and as we'll see today there is often science in the stories that they read!

After you've read the story and put the story disk on the map for the last time, turn to the illustration of the little boy catching Ping. Ask your student why he thinks the boy has a barrel on his back. He may or may not guess that it is for his safety. (You can teach a water safety lesson here, too.) Tell him that decades ago on the Yangtze River they didn't have life preservers and water wings the way we have today and the boy's parents wanted to be sure he was safe in the water!

Ask your student, "Do you want to know how the barrel works? Well, there is a really big word—you don't have to memorize it—but I thought you'd like to hear how it sounds. The word is *buoyancy*. Isn't that a funny word? Yes, I like the sound of it, too. Anyway, buoyancy means being able to float in a liquid." Your younger student will enjoy just sounding out this unusual word, while your older student may be interested in how it's spelled, as well! Continue with the lesson in the manual and find things that can be tested in a pan of water. Enjoy seeing which things float and which things don't. Use the activity sheet at the end of the Ping unit to document your student's experiments. He can then share this page with Dad, or Aunt, etc., and explain what he learned.

All of the above is an example of "inspired learning through great books," which is the cornerstone of the conversational presentation of the lessons in *Five in a Row*. The idea is to keep your lessons light, simple, exciting—through *your* voice and *your* interest in the subjects—and to engage in discussions, back and forth together, over

24

the various topics. Remember, too, that it is important to tie each lesson to the story through your conversation by saying things like, "Did you notice in our story today____" or "Have you ever thought of____ that happened in our story? Or, "When we read *The Story About Ping* today, I noticed that___," etc. Each lesson is included because it highlights something interesting in the story just waiting to be explored!

You may want to end your week with a meal that you make together from the *Five in a Row Cookbook* (at www.fiveinarow.com). Your student can use his knowledge of the week's story to name the various menu items. You'll find ideas for this activity in the cookbook. The end of the week celebration meal is a great time to cook together and set the table with related items from your story of the week. Invite a friend or extended family members and let your student share all the things he's learned during the week. There are special places for pictures of this event and for notes in your *Five in a Row Cookbook* that make this book a special keepsake of your times together, as well.

The *Five in a Row Christian Character and Bible Study Supplement* is another way to add to your week's learning activities. These are simple lessons on character that flow easily from the week's story unit. There are many lessons for each story to choose from and these lessons can be discussed at bedtime, in the car, on the weekend or anytime you'd like to fit one or more of them into your teaching times.

Important! Just because you are having conversations doesn't mean that your students don't create entries for the notebooks that they are keeping. Having a body of work to review and share with others is important. Information on notebook entries are part of each subject covered in "How to Use *Five in a Row*" in the front of each of your manuals. Activity pages at the end of each book unit are also provided as a way of documenting some of the lessons your student has learned. And you can find many supplemental notebooking ideas in the FIAR Notebook Builder at www.fiveinarow.com.

Reading the Stories Five Days in a Row

This section explains the reasoning and philosophy that went into creating lesson plans in which the story is read over and over (five days in a row). It details benefits and what to do if there is any resistance from your student.

Before you make a decision to read the selected story less than five days in a row, it may be helpful to know why the curriculum was developed this way. Then you have the background knowledge neccessary to decide how you want to use it with your student.

Some children read a story only for the plot. When they "know what has happened," they are ready for a new book. The plot is all they know to find in a book. It takes a bit of creativity and planning for these children to experience the richness of a good story—to find out how much more than just the plot can come to them through a great book!

Thus, the *Five in a Row* curriculum was designed to find many treasures in every story—across several academic topic areas—and to provide a built-in review every time you reread the story. Each day as your child hears the story again, he is saying to himself, "Oh, there is the personification!" or "Oh, I see how that artist balanced the picture...I remember that from yesterday." The *repeated opportunities* for your child to apply what he has learned as he hears the book over again is an important part of this curriculum.

In addition, each day as you read, your child will hear the sentence structure, syntax, mood and style of a story written by a great children's author. This repetitive reading of a story for five days can make a huge difference in your child's ability to read and write (at the proper time). His ear becomes used to good sentences—he may not have memorized them, but hearing them five times works almost as well. Again this will help in both reading and creative writing in the future.

Seeing the great works of art, five times in a row, in the illustrations of the *Five in a Row* selected titles, works in much the same way. Your student's eyes are being trained not to rush from one set of illustrations to another, but to observe different details each day as he listens to the book.

There truly was a great deal of thought that went into how this particular curriculum was created and structured, for the maximum benefits to occur. It isn't just a curriculum that recommends a book, has you read it once, and then moves you along.

Suggestions for a Resistant Student

Because there are significant benefits to reading the story over all five days, we have some suggestions for those who might have a more reluctant student. Read the story on the first day. The second day you can just say you are going to read it again, but this time you are going to leave out a part and see if they can catch you. (This technique is also good on day three or four.) Or you can add in a character or line and see if they can catch it!

Another day you can say that you are going to read the story again, but today your student can be looking for... (something in the art lesson you are going to do. For example, ask your student to look for every picture that has both orange and blue in it—since later that day you will do a lesson in complementary colors.)

You could also have your student draw something about the story while you are reading one day. This is not ideal, since they aren't looking at the pictures, but it's a good option for one day.

If you do a lesson on onomatopoeia one day, the next day have them listen for the examples and raise their hand or clap when they hear one. In this way, you are using the previous day's lessons to spur yet another reading of the book.

With the above ideas and approach, you are retaining the right to say what you will do for school in a gentle, friendly way: "This is what we are going to do," while at the same time caring for your student enough to create a helpful environment in which he can get over the hump of the problem, and learn to hear a good story for five days. Then you have a win-win situation.

I think you will find that after a few units, you won't have to do as much of this type of "leading" because your child will be used to reading the book five days in a row and he will actually be enjoying it!

All that said, you are the teacher and you will make the final decisions for your family on how to use FIAR. I just thought you might want to know why *Five in a Row* was created in this way and how this method will benefit your child's learning.

Blessings on all of your homeschool journey!
Jane Claire Lambert

The Bee Tree

Title:	*The Bee Tree*
Author:	Patricia Polacco
Illustrator:	Patricia Polacco
Copyright:	1993
Summary:	An adventure and a merry chase lead to a discovery about reading when Mary Ellen learns that good things take effort.

Social Studies: Relationships -Traditions

Grampa and Mary Ellen have a special relationship. (Notice that at the most exciting point of the bee chase Grampa gives the jar to Mary Ellen to let out the last bee!) They enjoy being with each other and Grampa shares with Mary Ellen the wisdom he's learned from his father and his father's father. Passing the information and skills we've learned to the next generation is often called carrying on the tradition of our elders.

Does your student's family have special traditions and special timing for events done through the generations? For instance, in one family it might be that on a child's fourteenth birthday his father opens a savings account for him, in the same way that his father did for him and his grandfather did for his father, etc. Many families and cultures have traditions that are handed down, as well as knowledge and skills.

Social Studies: Geography - Michigan and Yukon Territory, Canada

This story is set in the Michigan countryside. Michigan is considered an important tourist and manufacturing state in the Great Lakes region of the Midwest.

It borders four of the five Great Lakes and consists of two pieces of land called the upper and lower peninsulas. These two pieces of land are connected by the Mackinac (mack-i-naw) Bridge. See the map after the Science section and also in the activity sheets for this unit. Show your student how the state (the lower peninsula) is shaped like a mitten!

Detroit, Michigan is known for its automobile manufacturing, and farming is common in the state's lower peninsula. This area could well be the "countryside" of *The Bee Tree*. Another clue to location is found early in the story, when the bee heads "straight for the St. Joe River." The St. Joseph River is in southwest Michigan. Place the story disk in this area on your U.S. or world map.

Have your older student draw a picture of this unusual state from an atlas or reference book. If possible, label the Great Lakes. Talk about the definition of peninsula and notice the two peninsulas (upper and lower) that make up the state of Michigan. See the activity sheet at the end of this unit.

"Klondike" Bertha Fitchworth, just back from her expedition to the **Yukon**, brings up another area to explore. The Yukon (yoo-kahn) is a northwest Canadian territory. It was in the Klondike region of the Yukon that one of the greatest gold rushes took place, in 1897. Whitehorse is the capital city of this territory, rich in mineral wealth and magnificent scenery. You might even see a Royal Canadian Mounted Policeman here! Your older student might especially enjoy researching the **Mounties**, and learn much about Canada along the way. Search online or find a library book with other information on the **Klondike** region of the Yukon for the student who enjoys going on a "hunt" for more facts.

Social Studies: Culture

The colorful clothes, items in the home and the syntax of the characters in *The Bee Tree* suggest that these people are of eastern European origin. With your student, find text and illustrative clues to the cultural and geographic origins of these people. Examples: "Fast, you'll have to run", "This I would like to do, also", "To a bee tree we are going." The names may also give clues. Notice the clothes, hats, babushkas and bright scarves, etc. (**Teachers Note:** Syntax is the pattern of sentence structure. Different languages have different syntax and books originating in non-English cultures often sound peculiar to our "ear.")

Feduciary's "What ho? You're gonna scare me goats," sounds more western European—perhaps English or Irish.

Social Studies: Hospitality

Grampa and Mary Ellen share the chase and the honey with their neighbors, by inviting them all over for biscuits and fresh brewed tea. The people enjoy themselves and the break in their day. They even make time for music, dancing and storytelling.

Encourage your student to extend hospitality by letting him plan a small gathering of friends or family. He could choose a purpose, time, location, guest list and plan his own activities. If there is no special event to celebrate he could give a happy Monday party! Help him decide what to serve for refreshments. You could discuss how to greet people at the door, take their coats and serve them. Or your student might want to try hosting an outdoor party like Mary Ellen and her grampa.

Social Studies:
Relationships - Kindness to Animals

Grampa is careful not to hurt the bees when catching them. Feduciary Long-drop is worried that his goats will be scared by the stampede of people. In both of these cases, the characters were showing the wisdom of being kind to the animals (insects are classified as animals, belonging to the kingdom Animalia). Talk with your student about ways that he has noticed people being kind (or unkind) to their animals. Encourage him to think of ways to take good care of the animal life around him.

Language Arts: Catching the Clues

Ask your student, "what was your first clue that Grampa and Mary Ellen are off to an adventure?" (When Mary Ellen says they already have honey, her Grampa says, " ...but not like this." And, he answers her with a wink.) That wink is a clue that something unusual is about to happen. It adds enjoyment to his reading for your student to be looking for such clues. It is part of the fun of reading the details!

Learning to recognize signals (like Grampa's wink) while reading stories, helps your student become aware of such signals in real life. This increases his understanding and discernment of people and situations around him.

Language Arts: Onomatopoeia

(**Teacher's Note:** For those who have completed FIAR Vol. 1 and 2, your student may be pointing out this literary device to you when he hears you read the story. Watch and see if he remembers. If he doesn't, after a reading, you might ask, "When Einar Tundevold comes around the bend on his squeaky old bike, what sound do the wheels make?" [tweddle-tweddle-squeeeeeek] Then ask, "Do you remember the name of the literary device used here?" [Onomatopoeia (ahna-mahta-PEA-uh), a word that sounds like what it is describing—in this case a squeaky wheel.] For your older student, if he still doesn't remember then gently remind him again of the word and try using examples of this literary device during the day for review. (Onomatopoeia is a literary device that writers enjoy using from time to time to bring sounds to their writing. Onomatopoeia is forming a word that actually *sounds* like the word it is describing, as the buzz of a bee or the *clippity cloppety* of horses hooves.)

The wheels of Einar Tundevold's old bike went tweddle-tweddle-squeeeeeeek. Can you hear that old bike? And the crowd of assorted people went slap, bump, honk, tweddle-tweddle-squeak fump! Patricia Polacco has used onomatopoeia to bring sounds of life to her story. Your student can have fun inventing words that sound like what they are describing (the sound effects of literature!) and using onomatopoeia in his own work.

Language Arts: Vocabulary

junction   The meeting of two things, especially where roads cross.

foursome   A group of four people.

pitch(ed)   In this story, it means leaning far to one side. It is used in this same way when talking about boats and ships that are tossed side to side on the waves. You may discuss other uses of this word related to baseball, camping (pitch a tent), or the black tar-like sealants used on boats, etc.

pollen   The yellow powder that comes from the stamens of flowers and clings to the legs of bees.

charming   Describing the Hermann sisters; nice, lovely, enjoyable.

eureka   An exciting discovery. It means literally, "I have found it!" in Greek.

sprint   To run quickly for a short time.

stampede   A frenzied rush of people and/or animals.

chortled   A funny kind of throaty laughter, something like a chuckle.

hollow   A small valley between mountains.

bluff   A steep promontory, riverbank or cliff.

wisdom   Using the knowledge that you gain for solving problems and making good choices.

Language Arts: Analogy

Grampa spooned some honey on the cover of Mary Ellen's book and told her it was like the sweetness to be found in the reading of the book. He said it sometimes took an adventurous search to find the sweetness in a book, just like the chase to the bee tree.

For your older student, explain Grampa's example of their search for the bee tree to show Mary Ellen the richness in a book is making an *analogy*: comparing one thing to another which is dissimilar. (Analogy is akin to simile and metaphor. But analogy compares more than two words or brief ideas. It compares concepts within the entire story.)

Art: Musicians and Instruments

Part of the culture of the people in this Michigan countryside includes music and dancing. How many musical instruments can your student find in the pictures and text of the story? (Feduciary Longdrop's flute and a violin, a viola and a string bass, also called a double bass or simply bass)

Violins, violas, cellos and basses make up the string section of an orchestra. In this story, there are only three stringed instruments. Three instruments or voices playing or singing together are called a trio.

Art: Enjoying the Details

Ask your student to study the pictures and point out interesting details that he sees. Details might include: Grampa changing hats before he goes outside, the unusual blue heater on the first page, the half-visible picture on the wall beside the bookcase and the small portrait pictures on page one (and again on the next to last page), etc. There are many wonderful details in Polacco's vibrantly colored pictures, including **shapes**, **patterns** and **textures**.

Look at the page where Grampa catches the bees in the jar. The expressions on the faces of Grampa and Mary Ellen are different. Can your student describe them? (Grampa's face is pleased—he knows what he is doing, while Mary Ellen's face is full of wonder. This wonder is illustrated by her wide open eyes, while his are much more closed.)

Notice Mrs. Govlock in the red-orange cape pushing the baby carriage. She first appears on the page where Grampa catches the bees, in the background. Turn the page and she's up close! Follow her and notice what the baby is doing in each succeeding page.

Patricia Polacco has placed great importance on books and reading in *The Bee Tree*. Have your student examine the title and dedication pages, the first page and the last two pages of the book. Notice the importance of books and reading. Also, notice the change in Mary Ellen's attitude between the title page and the last page.

Art: Making a Map

For fun, try making a map with your older student of the path followed by Grampa and Mary Ellen and all their neighbors. Patricia Polacco uses colorful names to describe the path. Use them on your map: the cornfield, the creek way, Dietz Junction, St. Joe River, Bird Talk Fellow Ridge, Greiner's Bluff, Bishop's Meadow, Dead Man's Tree, Bird Talk Hollow, and Dunk's Woods. Making a map provides a good opportunity to talk about the terms: bluff, hollow, ridge, woods, meadow, junction, river, creek, etc. Drawing each one helps your student understand the term and remember it. Add the map to your student's notebook. Encourage him to watch for and point out such geographic features whenever you are on an outing.

Math: Hexagons

See if you can obtain a small piece of honeycomb from the grocery store. Let your student examine it. See what observations he makes. Remind your student that the honeycomb is comprised of hexagons (six equal-sided polygons) and let him see for himself. Bees, their activities and their honeycombs are all part of the immense wonder of creation! (The Michigan state rock called a Petoskey stone has hexagonal-like markings, too! Show your students a picture of this unique stone online.)

Science: Bees and Beekeeping

A field trip to actually see beehives is a wonderful and worthwhile project. Your student may have the opportunity to watch the smoking of the bees, which calms them so work can be done on the hives and some of the honey harvested. (Some has to be left for the bees!) If you're really lucky, you might even get a chance to see the bees swarming. Bees swarm when a hive grows too large and a new queen has matured. The new queen flies to a nearby tree branch and thousands of bees crowd around her. They must be scooped into a clean empty hive or they will fly away to search for a bee tree! A field trip may also give your student the opportunity to taste honeycomb straight from the hive and take home a jar of honey to enjoy in the winter.

Bees are truly fascinating creatures. Find a children's book on bees at the library, or look online for related topics such as bee anatomy and life cycle, types of bees, what goes on in a beehive, pollination and bees' usefulness to human beings, etc.

Science: Gold

"Klondike" Bertha's name reminds us of gold found in the Klondike region of the Yukon. Gold is a gigantic subject that could be a complete year's unit study by itself. Briefly, gold is a metallic* element** that comes from the earth and is made valuable by its relative scarcity. On the Periodic Table of Elements gold has the symbol Au. Just to hear the sound of the words gold, metal, element, Periodic Table of Elements, Au, is enough for your young student. You may wish to help him with a page on gold for his notebook. Let him print out or draw pictures of things made of gold, watches, rings, etc., to include on the page. It might look something like this (but done in his own way of course):

For your older student there are many topics to explore, including:

• The properties of the element gold (such as the ability to be hammered thin, or pulled into a thin wire)
• The mining of gold
• The value of gold on the market
• Things made from gold
• Gold rushes in history
• Exploration of countries and the search for gold
• The ancient civilizations and their use of gold
• Gold mentioned in the Bible

- Fort Knox
- Gold leaf
- Gold ingots
- Gold dental fillings
- The hidden gold in the story of *Treasure Island*
- The Gold Coasts of Australia, Africa and Florida
- Sayings like "good as gold," "heart of gold," "all that glitters is not gold," "silence is golden," etc.
- Stories like *The Goose That Laid the Golden Egg*, *Rapunzel* where the little man spins the hay into gold, and the mythological King Midas who had the golden touch

There is also a common understanding that gold stands for excellence. A gold medal or statue is given to the to first place winners in contests. Gold is considered synonymous with the highest and the best: a golden moment or a golden opportunity. Gold is also associated with longevity: Golden Years, Golden Wedding Anniversary, Golden Age.

(***Metal**: a category of elements that are shiny, and are good conductors of heat and electricity, and other qualities.) (****Element**: A substance composed of atoms having the same number of protons in each nucleus. Elements cannot be reduced to simpler substances by normal chemical means.) **Teacher's Note:** *Use only the bits of information that create a sense of wonder and interest for your student!*

Map of Michigan

Upper Peninsula

Lower Peninsula

The Mitten

Teacher's Notes

The *Five in a Row* lesson options for each unit in the manual are all you need to teach your child. The additional resource area provided below is simply a place to jot down relevant info you've found that you might want to reference.

THE BEE TREE

Date: _____

Student: _____

Five in a Row Lesson Topics Chosen:

Social Studies:
_____
_____
_____

Language Arts:
_____
_____
_____

Art:
_____
_____
_____

Math:
_____
_____
_____

Science:
_____
_____
_____

**Relevant Library Resources:
Books, DVDs, Audio Books**

_____
_____
_____
_____
_____
_____

Websites or Video Links:

_____
_____
_____
_____
_____
_____
_____

Related Field Trip Opportunities:
_____
_____
_____

Favorite Quote or Memory During Study:
_____
_____
_____

Name:

Date:

Math: **Hexagons**

See if you can obtain a small piece of honeycomb from the grocery store. Let your student examine it. See what observations he makes.

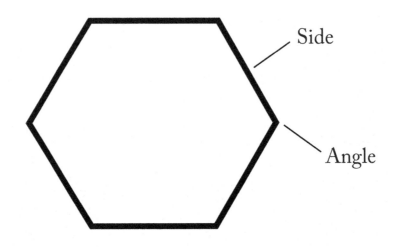

1. How many sides does a hexagon have? _____

2. How many angles does a hexagon have? _____

Did you know?

In honeycomb each side of a hexagon connects to other sides of hexagons. Draw more hexagons that attach to the ones below.

Name:

Date:

Social Studies: **Geography - Michigan**

After reading the lesson in the manual, color and label the map below.

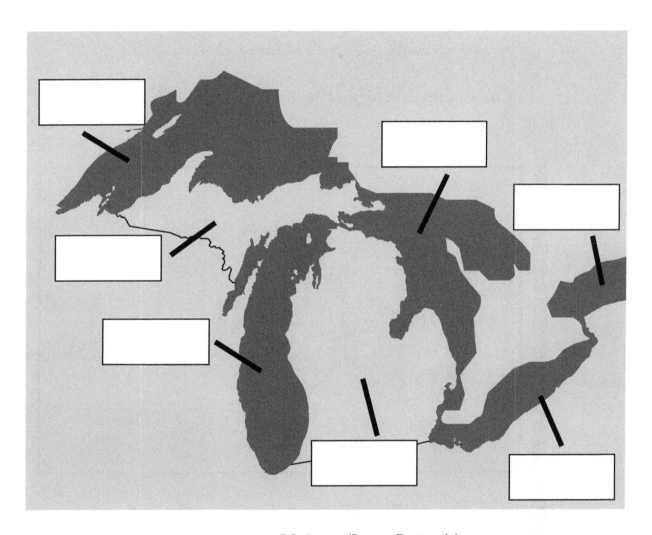

Michigan (Lower Peninsula)

Upper Peninsula

Lake Superior

Lake Huron

Lake Ontario

Lake Erie

Lake Michigan

Name:

Date:

Geography: **Michigan Flag**

The flag of Michigan has a dark blue field with the state's coat of arms in the center. The state coat of arms depicts a blue shield with a man holding a long gun representing the fight for state and nation. The elk and moose represent the great animals of Michigan. The bald eagle represents the United States. *For more information, see Parts of a Flag on page 224.*

Color in the Michigan flag below.

38

Andy and the Circus

Title:	*Andy and the Circus*
Author:	Ellis Credle
Illustrator:	Ellis Credle
Copyright:	1971
Summary:	Humor, helpfulness, a dream, sacrifice, and industry roll into a collision of a good story!

Teacher's Note: *Andy and the Circus* contains two instances where children, afraid of consequences, go behind their parents' back to save their pets. This is not the main part of the story line, and the story itself is one of industry, helpfulness and sacrifice. It is written by Ellis Credle, the author of *Down Down the Mountain*, FIAR Vol. 2, and displays the same values of hard work and real sacrifice found in that story. The FIAR lessons *do* address the issue of the children and their pets, but you may feel better by prereading the book and the following lesson suggestions to decide for yourself.

[While this selection is a story picture book, it takes longer to read than most FIAR selections.]

Social Studies: Relationships - Friends and Family

Andy has several friends: Joe (with the kittens), Mildred (with Miss Melissa, her doll), Bill (with the great jumping bullfrog and tadpoles) and Jeff (with the extraordinary trained pig, Sukey). Andy helps each one of them, along with many of his family members, even when it looks like his dream of seeing the circus will never come to pass. This is called "sacrifice" and he portrays it well.

Andy's family has lots of relatives. Can your student name some of them? (Andy's mother and father, his Grandpa and Grandma, and Aunt Minnie.) Place the story disk anywhere your student chooses, since there's no "real" geographic location given in the story.

(**Teacher's Note:** The following lesson point is ideally *self-taught*, as your student explores the book. These points are just for teacher's reference.)

What does the author show about Andy and his daily life with his family? (Andy cheerfully brings home ice and plow points for his parents; does his chores, like emptying the drip pan and feeding the mule; and he brings home candy for Grandpa. Even though he wants to go to the circus more than anything, he respects the way his parents are saving for things they need and does not ask them for ticket money. When his Grandpa refuses to help and suggests he "make his own way," Andy acts on the suggestion instead of being grumpy or mad.)

Social Studies: Relationships - Greed and Communication

Andy's friend Joe makes problems for himself by his greed. Can your older student figure out how this is so? (Andy asks Joe if he can have a kitten, and Joe says," No ... I want every single one." If Joe had been less greedy and found homes for his kittens, he would not have been frightened when his mother asked his father to take them to the mill.)

In addition, Joe only thought his mother intended to get rid of them. A mill is a place where many people come daily to get grain ground into flour, like the corn being ground into cornmeal in this story. Perhaps she expected the miller would find homes for the kittens among the many people visiting the mill. Joe, however, is afraid his father might be planning to drown them in the millpond and concludes that passing off the kittens to Andy is the *only* way to save them. (Mills can also be sawmills which cut wood or steel mills which convert iron ore into cast steel pieces.)

A little communication (asking questions and talking things out) might have helped this situation, saving Joe from being frightened and taking the kittens without permission. Whenever one is tempted to do something she thinks is wrong, she needs to remember that there is always more than one way to handle the situation. Sometimes one feels she must do something that is wrong to accomplish what she desires because she thinks it's the only way. That "*only way*" phrase is a danger signal that should always capture our attention. Again, there is almost always more than one way to handle the situation, and good communication skills can bypass a multitude of problems.

Also, while Joe is greedy with his kittens, Andy portrays the opposite character quality as he continues to help people, even though he is running out of time to get his job at the circus.

Social Studies:
Transition to the Industrial Age

This story captures an interesting period in the history of this country as people were beginning to "modernize" by using more gasoline-powered and electrical equipment and appliances. But these new appliances cost more, and money had to be saved in order to purchase them, often over long periods of time.

(It might make an enjoyable combination to coordinate the reading of this story with lessons on chores and saving.)

Ask your student if she could imagine having to haul ice and empty drip pans daily. Talk about the temperature fluctuations of the old "ice box" and the shorter time period in which food could safely be kept. You might also discuss the shortage of space compared to today's modern refrigerators. And, of course, we don't have to add ice or empty the drip pan in today's units, either.

Ask your student if she would rather walk behind a mule and plow or drive a tractor. There are both benefits and problems with each "new" product. Discuss some of each. Mules don't create the same kind of pollution problems as tractors and the ice box is not affected by a power outage, etc. But refrigerators have many benefits and a tractor is certainly faster than a mule!

Grandpa offers a stereotypical view of many of the older people during the time that the new machines were "new-fangled gadgets." In his case, the wisdom of using the mower for a form of exercise makes sense. But many older people were afraid to use the new devices, or felt that the old ones were just as good. These feelings are still common today. Can you thinks of areas today where this is true? (Computers, space travel, microwave ovens, cruise control, social media, etc.)

Through studying *Andy and the Circus*, your young student will get just a taste of this historic "time of desire" for modern machinery. However, your older student may want to find out more about the challenges and benefits of this time period of change as people were getting electric lighting and appliances, and beginning to use machinery powered by gasoline and electricity. Encourage her to explore some of these topics. (Remember that the cities were always ahead of the rural areas in these transitional times of modernizing change.)

Language Arts: Details

Andy comes riding into the story with a plow point on the back of his bicycle, a block of ice in the front basket and some horehound candy in his pocket. Ask your student to match these items with the correct family members. Andy wants to ask these same three people for help to purchase a ticket. Follow through with the reasons why this doesn't work. (Andy's mother used the block of ice for her ice box, but she was saving her money for a new refrigerator. So Andy didn't ask her.

Andy's father used the new plow point to plow his field, but he was saving his money for a new tractor. Andy didn't ask him either. His grandpa did not want a new power mower, but he believed that children should *work* for what they want and sent him to the circus for a job.)

Language Arts: Idioms and Sayings

On the wall beside the icebox is a framed saying, "The way to a man's heart is through his stomach." Ask your student if she can figure out what this means. Why would this saying be in the *kitchen*? If your student enjoys these kind of sayings, introduce her to some of Benjamin Franklin's witticisms from *Poor Richard's Almanac*: Early to bed and early to rise makes a man healthy, wealthy and wise; a stitch in time saves nine, etc.

Art: Negative Effect

Look at the illustrations for *Andy and the Circus*. Except for the cover picture, the illustrations are all one color: blue. This is the same monochrome (one color) type of illustration used in *Lentil* (FIAR Vol. 1) and *Make Way for Ducklings* (FIAR Vol. 2), both by Robert McCloskey. The double page illustration right before the picture of Andy falling with all the things around him, is blue ink on white paper. Find this picture and study it carefully. Then turn to the picture on the inside cover of the book. This picture is a negative of the former, with the white areas shown in blue and the blue areas in white. If your older student would like, have her draw two circus pictures as much alike as possible. On one, have her use white paper and a blue colored pencil, crayon or paint. On the other give her blue paper with white pencil, chalk or paint. She could even try simple circus posters!

Perhaps you, your parents, or even grandparents have some old photographs taken with film and their corresponding negatives. Let your student examine them, noting how they are exact opposites of one another.

Art: Method for Clouds

Ellis Credle has used a special method for creating the effect of clouds in the sky. Instead of painting white puffs on top of blue, or leaving out white spaces and painting solid blue around it, she has sketched small blue lines around the area she wishes to make stand out as clouds.

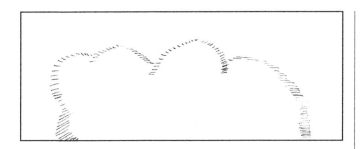

Try this technique and experiment with different ways to show a cloudy sky.

Art: Circus Posters and Circus Performers

Circus posters are exciting pieces of art that seek to sell the public the wonders of the show. On a large poster you will see bright colors, breathtaking pictures full of action, and dramatic phrases, all geared to excite the public and sell tickets. If your student is interested, let her design a poster for an exciting event and include color, action illustrations, and descriptive phrases in her work. The event may be real or imaginary.

The circus in this story takes place many years ago when circuses were somewhat different than they might be today. Make a list of all the different types of circus performers that you see in the story. Add any others that circuses may have now or in the past such as stilt walkers, lion tamers, acrobats, jugglers, high-wire walkers, elephant handlers, and clowns.

Clowns go to special clown schools. They develop a name, an act, a special outfit and makeup scheme. No two clowns have exactly the same makeup or costume. After graduating from clown school, the clowns take jobs in different circuses around the world and perform for many special functions. Learning about clowns and clown schools is an interesting research topic.

Art: Circus Train

In years past, and even in some areas of the world today the circus train would come into town and thrill the crowds with the colorful cars, clowns waving from the windows and an occasional glimpse of wild animals inside. The last illustration of the story shows a circus train curving across the double page. Find an oatmeal box for the engine and shoe boxes for the cars. Help your student make a colorful circus train and savor the old time excitement of the circus coming to town!

Math: Counting, Savings, and Salaries

Andy and the Circus provides opportunities for counting, such as animals, people, train cars, etc. For your older student this story can also be the catalyst for learning about saving money. Just as the adults in the story were saving for special items, you can discuss how saving works and project how much might be saved from a dollar a week allowance, etc. You could also have a discussion of salaries based on Andy's desire to have a job with the circus and project how much he might receive over the summer, etc.

Science: Balance

Since this story is about Andy and all the precariously balanced cargo on his bicycle, it might be a good time to introduce the concept of balance. If you have a balance scale, you might let your young student place items, such as pennies, on one side. Let her discover for herself that the same number of items placed on the other side make the scale come into balance. Try balancing unlike objects. For instance, a clothespin might be balanced by 8, 12 or 15 pennies. Your student can estimate how many it will take to balance and see how close she can come to guessing (estimating) the correct quantity.

Balance is also a function of design. You may have already explored balance as it applies in art and architecture through previous *Five in a Row* lessons. Buildings that have a balance of design often have the same number of windows on each side of the door, etc. Drawings can be balanced by a large figure on one side with several small figures on the other, etc.

In addition, balance can refer to a person's physical stance. People are balanced as they walk (or else they fall down). They can balance on one foot. (Some birds balance on one foot, too.) And people can balance things they carry in their hands or on their heads. Has your student ever seen photographs or videos of people in other countries balancing baskets or jugs of water on their head without using their hands? (We balance things every day too, such as a stack of dishes or books. Sometimes we reach our destination safely, but other times our point of balance is upset and the books or dishes come crashing down.) Riding a bicycle, skateboarding, skiing and many other activities require learning the skill of balance.

Just for fun, let your student try to balance as many things as she can and walk across the room. She could hold a tall stack of things (such as blocks) in her hands or try to balance something on her head. Try using stuffed toys, small notebooks or other unbreakables. Get a funny hat, under which some items can be hidden, and maybe she'll imagine herself a clown in the circus!

Science: Frogs and Tadpoles

Frogs are **amphibians** and have an amazing life cycle. That is why the scoutmaster wanted to show his boys the wondrous tadpoles. The eggs hatch in the water and small animals emerge with large tails, no legs, and no lungs; they breathe through gills. They look nothing like frogs! Which is exactly why Andy said, "Baby frogs? They don't look like frogs!" As they mature, the tail begins to disappear and legs grow. Eventually, the lungs are formed, the tail is gone and the legs are big and strong. The frog is now ready for its life on land. See the "Amphibious Life Cycles" page at the end of this unit.

In the spring, if you can find a pond, look for masses of eggs at the pond's edge. They are almost clear and you have to look carefully. If you can, obtain a few eggs and set up a small freshwater aquarium in which to raise tadpoles. Tadpoles can be raised on certain types of granular fish food from pet stores. When the frogs are mature, they can be released near the pond from which they came. On your trip to the pond, find a shaded spot, read the story again and have a picnic lunch of cornbread with a ham slice and some watermelon for dessert! Now isn't this a fun way to learn?

(**Teacher's Note:** Amphibians are explained more completely in *The Salamander Room* lessons. Also, the suggestions for making games in *The Salamander Room* lesson entitled Science: Classification of the Animal KingdomVertebrates could be applied to this lesson. Remember, the wonder of seeing a tadpole turn into a frog is more important at this age level than intense memorization of the facts surrounding the event. Lay bits and pieces of information out there in an informal way, and what is caught is fine and what is not has at least been introduced.)

Teacher's Notes

The *Five in a Row* lesson options for each unit in the manual are all you need to teach your child. The additional resource area provided below is simply a place to jot down relevant info you've found that you might want to reference.

ANDY AND THE CIRCUS

Date: _____

Student: _____

Five in a Row Lesson Topics Chosen:

Social Studies:
_____
_____
_____

Language Arts:
_____
_____
_____

Art:
_____
_____
_____

Math:
_____
_____
_____

Science:
_____
_____
_____

Relevant Library Resources: Books, DVDs, Audio Books
_____
_____
_____
_____
_____
_____
_____
_____

Websites or Video Links:
_____
_____
_____
_____
_____
_____
_____
_____

Related Field Trip Opportunities:
_____
_____
_____

Favorite Quote or Memory During Study:
_____
_____
_____

46

Amphibious Life Cycles

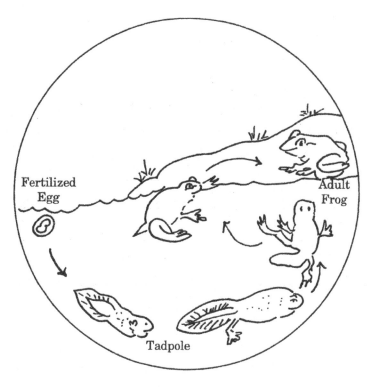

Frogs and Tadpoles

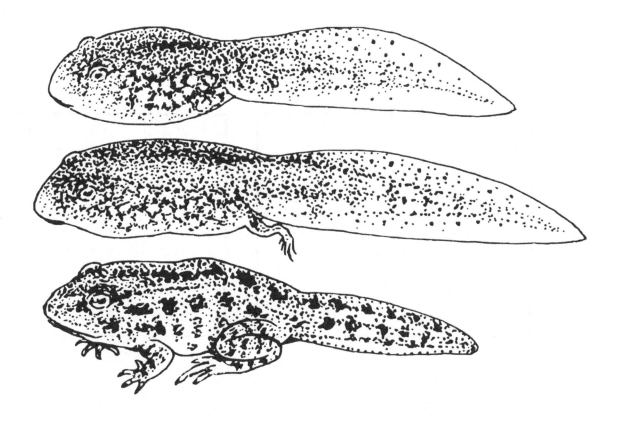

Name:

Date:

Art: **Method for Clouds**

Ellis Credle has used a special method for creating the effect of clouds in the sky. Instead of painting white puffs on top of blue, or leaving out white spaces and painting solid blue around it, she has sketched small blue lines around the area she wishes to make stand out as clouds.

Use the frames below to try different ways to show clouds; making a least one in the same style as Andy and the Circus.

Name:

Date:

Science: **Balance**

Here are a few different ways to experiment with balance. Try these ideas and draw or take notes of your results, or answers to the questions below, on a separate sheet of paper. Dictation is a great way for younger children to answer these questions while thinking quickly and letting you do the work of writing it down. Pair the answers with this question page and file in your notebook under Science.

1. Balance on One Foot

First try standing on one foot and balancing. Next, stand on one foot but try holding a heavy object with one hand (a gallon of milk, or bag of rice, etc.). Notice how you have to lean your body to the opposite side to balance the additional weight. What are you doing by leaning to the opposite side of the heavy object? What happens if you don't lean or pull your body in the opposite direction? What else could you do to balance the weight? (answer: hold a similar item in the other hand)

2. Make a Balance Scale

Search online for ways to make a DIY or homemade balance scale. There are many variations and this could be a great project to tackle together and provide a wonderful learning opportunity. Then you can gather objects to weigh, perhaps guessing which one will be heavier before placing them on the scale.

3. Teeter-Totter (at the park)

The definition of balance is an even distribution of weight. As you learned with balancing on one foot while holding a heavy object and practicing with a balance scale (if you made one), having a heavier object on one side makes the weight uneven and one side drops lower than the other side. How does a teeter-totter work like a balance scale? Does it work if one person weighs a great deal more than the other? What could you do to balance it out? (Possible answers could include, doubling up children on one side to be closer to a parent's weight on the other side. Or, having a parent hold some of their weight up off of the seat to make themselves lighter and therefore closer to their child's weight.)

The Wild Horses of Sweetbriar

Title:	*The Wild Horses of Sweetbriar*
Author:	Natalie Kinsey-Warnock
Illustrator:	Ted Rand
Copyright:	1990
Summary:	Hardships of a cold winter make memories to last a lifetime with the wild horses of Sweetbriar.

Social Studies: Geography - Nantucket

Although based on a true incident, it is assumed that Sweetbriar is a fictitious name for an island off the coast of another well known island, Nantucket. Nantucket Island is a real place, off the coast of Massachusetts. Historically the large island of Nantucket was known for whaling, basket making, and a hardy people who saw themselves as special and rather independent, and the rest of the people in the U.S. as "mainlanders."

Massachusetts is one of the New England states. *Cranberry Thanksgiving*, FIAR Vol. 1, contains a lesson on New England. The upper east coast of the United States and Canada has rocky shoreline requiring lighthouses. In the past, brave and committed men (and a few women), like the father in this story, ran the lighthouses. Today, nearly all of them are automated.

For a great go-along book about one of those few women lighthouse keepers, read *The Bravest Woman in America* by Marissa Moss. Another wonderful title that supplements lighthouse education but from a different perspective is *Lightship* by Brian Flocca.

Place your story disk near Nantucket Island, and discuss the name of the ocean to the east of the United States and Canada: the Atlantic Ocean.

Social Studies: Assateague and Chincoteague, Virginia, Islands of Wild Horses

Though *The Wild Horses of Sweetbriar* is based on a true incident that happened off the coast of Massachusetts, there is a place in Virginia where you can still see wild ponies on an island. Assateague (ASS-uh-teeg) Island has wild ponies that increase each season. In July, some of these ponies are driven across the water to Chincoteague (CHING-kuh-teeg) Island for the annual roundup. Your older student, especially a horse lover, might enjoy further research on this topic.

Social Studies: Living in Isolation

After reading the story through, discuss with your student the pros and cons of living isolated from other people. Talk about how it affected the mother (she was extremely lonely and missed family, friends and the niceties of town life, shops, churches, etc.). Also, talk about how it affected the little girl (she was exhilarated by the island with its smells, sights and the horses that she loved). Does your student think it would have been good for the child if she had lived on Sweetbriar Island for many years? What might she have been like and what benefits or problems might she have had? (No right or wrong answers here, just wondering and discussion.) Has your student ever had to be isolated from others for a period of time? What are his memories of that time? Or, you can share your memories with him if he hasn't had this particular experience.

Language Arts: Using a True Incident

This story is based on a true incident on the island of Tuckernuck in 1865. Natalie Kinsey-Warnock decided to reset the story in 1903 and change the name of the island to Sweetbriar. Your older student may find this fact interesting and understand that he, too, can take an incident and "reset" the time, place and characters. If he wishes he may use only the *framework* of the event for inspiration. Add "Fictionalizing A True Event" to your list of Choices a Writer Can Make.

Language Arts: Point of View

The Wild Horses of Sweetbriar is written from the first person point of view. Ask your student if he remembers how **first person point of view** sounds. (The story is told from an "I" point of view: "In the summer of 1903, when I was almost eight ..." The girl who tells the story does not happen to reveal her name, although many stories told in first person say something like, "**I** waited all summer for **my** new bike. **My** name is Annie and **I** love to ride. One day ...")

Using the pronouns I, me, my, etc., your older student may want to try writing a story or remembrance of his own. He could also try writing a short paragraph in first person, and then rewriting it in third person, using he, they, his own name, etc.

Language Arts: Poetic Device - Simile

If your student has completed FIAR Vols. 1 and 2, ask him if he knows what a simile is. If he isn't sure, explain that a **simile** compares two unlike things using words of comparison such as like, as, seems, etc.

There is a simile in the fourth paragraph of the first page of *The Wild Horses of Sweetbriar*. Reread this last sentence of the fourth paragraph and notice that it was the "smell" of the wild roses and sea that was so thick the girl could have *spread it like jam*. Or more simplified: the smell was thick like jam.

The next page of text says, "They [the horses] flew across the sand **like** windblown seeds ... ," a simile comparing the horses' swift travel to windblown seeds. When the snow fell in November, the text says, "the wind blew the snow so hard it felt **like** needles." This is another example of simile.

Teacher's Note: In the same sentence cited above, the phrase, "their dark hooves splashed stars from the sea" is a metaphor. A metaphor is similar to a simile but does not use words of comparison such as like or as. In this case the spray thrown up by the horses hooves was said to be stars, not *like* stars but to actually *be* stars (meaning sparkling), making the phrase metaphoric.

Art: Line of Design

The Wild Horses of Sweetbriar has single illustrations that cover the width of two pages. Find the third illustration of the story, where the wild horses are running through the surf. Ask your student to locate the girl who loves horses. (She's at the top of the hill.) Now talk about the triangular line of design with the horses across the foreground of the picture and the girl and tree on the hilltop. If your student is interested, let him compose a picture with a similar line of design.

Art: Use of Light

On Christmas Eve, when the girl and her Mama heard the noises outside, they opened the door to find hungry horses, "eyes glinting red in the light." Ted Rand, the illustrator, uses yellow for the light of the home pouring through the door at night. This yellow color is reflected in the faces of the horses. If your student completed FIAR Vol. 1, remind him of the yellow light from the windows at night in *Papa Piccolo*. By reviewing the artist's technique to make light appear at night, your student will again see that he can also choose yellow for light in his dark night pictures.

The red glint in the horses' eye is caused by a reflection of direct light from the back of the horses' eyeball due to the fact that the pupil of the eye is widely dilated from the dark. If you have any photographs of people or pets with "red eye," share them with your student and explain that many cameras now have a pulsing light prior to the flash that helps prevent this phenomenon from occurring. The pulsing light causes the pupil of the eyes to constrict just before the flash goes off.

Art: Comparison

If you own a copy of *Cranberry Thanksgiving*, compare the first picture of the *Cranberry* book to the fourth picture of *Sweetbriar*. Note the similarities and remember that they both take place in New England. (Overcast leaden sky, both girls gathering driftwood for the fire, the black-stockinged birds at the water, and the long marsh grasses.) If you get a chance to travel to the New England area, your student will be interested to see places that actually look like these pictures!

Also, compare the first pictures of healthy horses to the later starving ones. Ask your student how the artist showed the horses were not well. (They were very thin—you can see their ribs. Their legs are even more fragile looking than in the first pictures, and their heads are constantly drooping.)

The ability to compare pictures, noticing similarities and differences, while thinking about the reasons for them are important skills for your student as he learns to explore art. This is the beginning of the road that leads him to notice, think for himself and learn from his own observations.

Art: Spattering for Effect

Throughout the pictures of *The Wild Horses of Sweetbriar*, Ted Rand, the illustrator, uses white paint spattered on top of what appears to be dried watercolor painting (or maybe some acrylic) to show both sprays of surf and falling snow. If your set of watercolors doesn't include white, obtain a tube of white watercolor paint. Let your student paint a watercolor picture with background and sky and whatever figures he chooses. When it is dry, mix some of the white paint and a very little water. Show him how to spatter it onto his painting with an old toothbrush. (It works well to hold the toothbrush, handle in hand, and use the thumb to pull back the brush bristles. As the bristles are let go, they spatter the paint forward onto the paper. You might want to let him practice first on a piece of black construction paper before he tries it on his painting.) This is one technique that artists use to put white "on top" of paint. Add "Spattering For Effect" to your list of Choices an Artist Can Make.

Also notice the white on the waves of certain pictures. There are some very good wave treatments to imitate in the geese flying picture and in the picture with the "ghost" horse memories, as well as the last picture. If your student thinks these waves look interesting (and different from other paintings he has seen), let him look carefully at the colors Mr. Rand uses and also try to imitate the action of the waves. Remember, your student may need to let the painting dry in between colors to gain the effect he desires.

Art: Depicting Memories or Dreams

There are many ways to capture the idea of a memory or dream, but the double page picture before the last page is an excellent example to bring to your student's attention. In this picture you see the little girl sitting in the foreground on a little hill with her back to the reader. Does this give your student the impression that she is not paying attention to anything other than her *own* thoughts? What is she doing? (She is remembering her wonderful, exciting wild horses and seeing them again in her memory.)

In this same type of picture format your student can show things that he's seen, or dreamed or imagined, with himself somewhere in the foreground and his thoughts outlined only *vaguely* (more lightly) in the sky. Put this idea on your list of Choices an Artist Can Make. Perhaps someday your student will remember the idea and use it when he needs it.

Math: Gallons, Quarts, Pints

Tie this math lesson into the story after you have read it through by showing your student the page where Papa arrives home and Mama is canning. Explain that putting up food for the winter often involves canning. One method of canning involves putting food in jars, sealing the jars with lids, and putting them in boiling water to kill any bacteria that causes spoilage in the food. The food will stay good in the jars for a long period of time. When you "can" food, you need to measure the ingredients and food carefully. The jars that are used for canning come in gallon sizes (often used for pickles), and in quarts, pints and half-pints.

For your young student, just show him a gallon jar (or a milk jug) and tell him the name "gallon," a quart jar and say, "This is a quart jar," etc. You may also let him see how many pint jars of water it takes to fill a gallon or quart, just for the fun of it, but not to memorize the information.

For your older student, show him how to calculate how many pints in a quart, quarts in a gallon, pints in a gallon, etc.

And if your younger student has not read Robert McCloskey's *Blueberries for Sal*, find a copy and enjoy Sal's exciting adventure involving putting up food for the winter!

[**Teacher's Note:** Besides canning, another way to preserve food is drying (or sometimes smoking). The father in this story dries cod to use in the winter. In *Down Down the Mountain*, FIAR Vol. 2, the family dried shucky beans to preserve them.]

Math: Counting by Tens

After reading the story through, ask your older student how many horses the girl saw on the island. (Ten) Now ask how many there would be if there were twice that many, three times, four times, etc. Show him how these answers are the same as counting by tens and have him count by tens as high as he can.

Science: Flora and Fauna

Flora (the plants of a particular area) and fauna (the animals of a particular area) are probably unfamiliar words for your young student. To introduce him to such big concepts, take an index card and write" **flora**" (saying the word for him) and let him decorate it by drawing or gluing on pictures of plants. Now make another card for "**fauna**" (saying the word for him, FAW-na). Let him draw or glue pictures of animals on the card. He just may enjoy the *sound* of these unusual words, and with the help of the pictures, pick up the terminology just for fun. Your older student can make his own index card and illustrate it and then list the flora and fauna of the Sweetbriar New England island area for his notebook. The following list contains examples of the flora and fauna of the Sweetbriar region.

Flora	Fauna
Blueberry bushes	**Wood ducks**
Wild rice	**Geese**
Wildflowers	**Wild horses** (various types)
Beach plums	**Gulls**
Wild roses	(**Cormorant**- a bird for which
Daisies	the island was named, not
Marsh grass	mentioned in the text)
Carrots	**Fish**: including cod
Various trees	

You can always make a game of it by asking your student to name different flora and fauna that he sees around him, and sometimes naming something yourself, saying, "Is it flora or fauna?" This is like the old guessing game "Animal, Vegetable or Mineral."

Science: Weathering

After reading the story, turn to the second page and repeat, "It was just a tiny house, made of shingles that the wind and sun had turned gray." Most books on New England will show pictures of weathered, gray houses (Cape Cod style homes) and many artists' pictures of this area have similar scenes. Talk about the harshness of the wind and salty sea air and the bleaching effects of the sun. Point out pictures online and from artists that depict this type of weathering process. Remind your student that when he sees these types of weathered, shingle board buildings along with the marsh grasses, etc., he may be looking at a picture of the New England area.

Different types of weathering processes take place in different climates. Be on the lookout for weathered buildings where your student lives and point them out. Also, you may find weathered pieces of driftwood along rivers or on beaches, etc. You can even find fences or wooden garden stakes which have been grayed and bleached by sun, wind and rain.

Science: Erosion

The little girl wanted to know how horses came to Sweetbriar Island. Ask your student if he can remember what her father said. (He said the island was once connected to Nantucket and that the horses must have come before the sea washed away the land in between.) Discuss erosion and point out areas that have dirt with deep gullies washed out by the rain.

Make a drawing to show your student how the small island could have been detached from the larger one by erosion.

Science: Bacteria

When Mama made the preserves, she had to protect the finished product from bacteria. Bacteria are microscopic single-celled organisms. While many bacteria are beneficial, some are harmful to humans and cause diseases. In the canning and freezing processes, care is taken to protect food from harmful bacterial growth. Canning jars are sterilized (rinsed with boiling water) to prevent bacterial growth in the food. Sometimes jars of preserves are covered with liquid paraffin which hardens and keeps the jellies from contact with the air and airborne bacteria.

Bacteria and germs are the reason you preserve some kinds of food (through canning, freezing or refrigeration) and why you wash your hands before preparing food and eating it. Perhaps you can discuss the importance of keeping hot foods hot and cold foods cold, washing your knives and cutting boards with hot soapy water after slicing poultry, etc.

56

Teacher's Notes

The *Five in a Row* lesson options for each unit in the manual are all you need to teach your child. The additional resource area provided below is simply a place to jot down relevant info you've found that you might want to reference.

THE WILD HORSES OF SWEETBRIAR

Date: _____

Student: _____

Five in a Row Lesson Topics Chosen:

Social Studies:
_____
_____
_____

Language Arts:
_____
_____
_____

Art:
_____
_____
_____

Math:
_____
_____
_____

Science:
_____
_____
_____

Relevant Library Resources: Books, DVDs, Audio Books

_____
_____
_____
_____
_____
_____
_____

Websites or Video Links:

_____
_____
_____
_____
_____
_____
_____
_____

Related Field Trip Opportunities:
_____
_____
_____

Favorite Quote or Memory During Study:
_____
_____
_____

Name:

Date:

Science: **Bacteria Experiment**

This experiment will show you how soap helps get rid of germs (bacteria is one type of germ).

You will need:

- a pie plate (or deep plate)
- water
- ground black pepper
- dishwashing liquid soap

Instructions:

Fill the plate with water to cover bottom. Sprinkle 1 tsp ground black pepper onto the water. Explain that the pepper represents germs/bacteria. Cover one of your fingers completely in dishwashing soap then put the soap-covered finger into the center of the peppery water. Observe what happens next and make notes below.

Name:

Date:

Math: **Gallons, Quarts, & Pints**

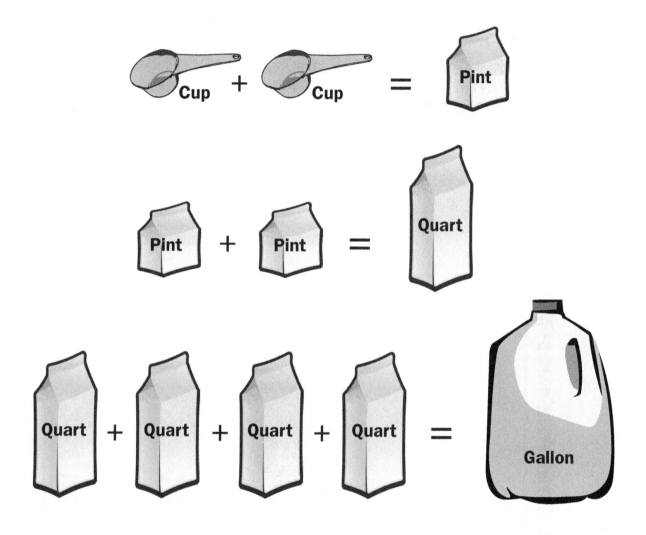

1. How many cups are in a pint? _____

2. How many pints are in a quart? _____

3. How many quarts are in a gallon? _____

4. How many pints are in a gallon? _____

Name:

Date:

Geography: **Massachusetts Flag**

The shield in the center of the flag of Massachusetts carries the image of an Algonquian Native American. A white star appears next to the figure's head, signifying Massachusetts as a U.S. state. A blue ribbon flows under the shield, with the state motto Ense Petit Placidam, Sub Libertate Quietem ("By the Sword We Seek Peace, But Peace Only Under Liberty"). Above the shield there is a bent arm holding a sword. This is meant to demonstrate that one would rather lose their right arm than live under tyranny. *For more information, see Parts of a Flag on page 224.*

Color in the Massachusetts flag below.

Paul Revere's Ride

Title: *Paul Revere's Ride*

Author: Henry Wadsworth Longfellow

Illustrator: Ted Rand (it is this illustrated edition of the poem that is being showcased)

Copyright: 1990

Summary: The exciting rendition of the ride of Paul Revere is made more vivid by Ted Rand's bold watercolor paintings.

Social Studies: History - Beginning of the American Revolution

Henry Wadsworth Longfellow has written a poem of an actual historic event. Poetry, like song, is an enjoyable way to learn and memorize pieces of historic information.

[**Teacher's Note:** It may be that Longfellow has taken a few liberties with the facts. Some historians say it was someone else who actually saw the two signal lights and reported to Paul Revere, and there may have been more riders involved in the warning. Poets and artists may focus on the most significant fact or figure to make an impact, sometimes at the expense of complete detailed facts. Longfellow may have taken the most prominent (well known) figure in the story and kept the facts to a minimum to simplify the poem. However, the importance of the ride and the bravery exhibited by Revere, as well as the others, is captured accurately in the verse.]

An easy way to visually peg the events of the ride of Paul Revere in early American history is to remember that his ride (April 18, 1775), took place after the Boston Tea Party (Dec. 16, 1773), but before the adoption of the Declaration of Independence on July 4, 1776. A page for your student's history section notebook might look something like this:

Boston Tea Party

December 16th, 1773

Paul Revere's Ride

April 18th, 1775

Declaration of Independence

July 4th, 1776

Just remembering the pictures will help keep the events in order even if each date is not fully memorized.

Social Studies: Geography - Boston

Paul Revere's ride began with a signal from the Old North Church in Boston in the colony of Massachusetts, which Paul intercepts from the Charlestown shore. He then continues past Charlestown, across the Mystic River, by Medford and on to Lexington. Place your story disk on Massachusetts.

There is a map in the front of the book that traces the ride, including two additional riders, Prescott and Dawes, who also spread the warning. The map does show direction (note north is slightly to the left of top), but it does not show the scale, making it difficult to tell how far it was from Charlestown to Medford or from Medford to Lexington.

Teacher's Information: It was about 16 miles from Boston to Lexington, where Revere and Dawes were stopped by British soldiers. Prescott made it through to Concord. The map on the inside cover also shows the two rivers in this area: the Charles and the Mystic which both flow into Boston Harbor. (Boston, Massachusetts is the town studied in *Make Way For Ducklings*, FIAR Vol. 2, although the time setting for the ducklings book was over 150 years later.)

Social Studies: History - The Use of Signals

The patriots in *Paul Revere's Ride* decided to use the belfry of the Old North Church and a lantern signal to alert Paul Revere and others to the movement of the British troops. They agreed to use one light for land movement and two if the British moved by water. The agreed signal worked and the minutemen were warned. (See **minutemen** in this story's vocabulary lesson.)

There are as many different kinds of signals as there are special needs for them. People have always invented ways of communicating secret information. It might be fun to brainstorm with your older student. Compile a giant list of secret communication methods and how they were used. The list might include: smoke signals, written codes, lights, flags, Morse code, pebbles thrown at a window, bird calls, animal calls, gunshots, tree carvings, flares and mirrors. In the movie *Anne of Green Gables*, Anne and Diana had a code worked out by raising and lowering the window shades to signal each other. In a Bible story, a scarlet cord was used as a signal (Joshua, chapter 2), as well as three arrows (1 Samuel, chapter 20), and the list goes on. Make a list of all the types of signals you've ever heard of or seen used.

With your young student, make up a secret code. (Remind your student that anything people agree upon can be used for a signal.) It can be as short as one word to signal her to do something, or perhaps a hand signal that you have both noticed something. It could be that you wear a certain pin or scarf on days when a special event will take place. Like an animal pin for zoo trips, etc. You could also create a simple code or signal that can be sent by flashlight and try it out in a dark place. And if you remember special signals you used as a child and the adventures you had with them, be sure to share these stories with your student. The world of codes and signals is interesting, entertaining, historic and creative.

Language Arts: Reading Poetry Aloud

This story poem provides an opportunity to strengthen poetry reading skills. If you are not familiar with reading poetry out loud, you may enjoy looking over the poetry reading tips before you present *Paul Revere's Ride* to your student.

1. Read the poem out loud, remembering that you never stop automatically at the end of each line. Rather, you follow the punctuation. Some lines may end with a comma, etc., but many lines will have no ending punctuation. Therefore, try continuing without a definite breath or stop until you reach a comma, period, etc.

Listen my children, and you shall hear
Of the midnight ride of Paul Revere.

These lines are read:
"Listen my children and you shall hear of the midnight ride of Paul Revere."

It's all one complete sentence.

On the first page, the word "alive" in line four goes on without a pause to line five. You may speed up or slow down your voice (without definite pauses at the ends of the lines) in order to avoid a sing-song rhythm of reading.

2. When you are comfortable with the knowledge of where to pause and breathe in the reading of the poem, then read it out loud all the way through just to hear the rhythm and sound of the words. Listen for rhyming or alliteration (same sounds at the beginnings of words), etc. Just hear and enjoy the rhythm and sound.

3. Read the poem again to understand it. A second reading will clarify the time, setting, historic significance and what the poem actually says.

4. Then, put it all together: reading the poem well out loud, enjoying the sounds playing upon each other, and understanding the meaning of the work. Enjoy it!

[**Teacher's Note:** Your young student will benefit from hearing the story poem and she will learn to enjoy the sounds and cadences. The more poetry she hears, the more she will enjoy, and the more she will begin to understand what makes a good poem. If you have an older elementary student, you may want to teach her some of the poetry-reading tips.]

Language Arts: Italics - Names of Ships

With this historic poem you find the name of an actual ship of history: the *Somerset*, a British man-of-war. Ask your student why this word *Somerset* seems to be in different type. If she knows, congratulate her! If not, remind her that the names of ships are set into a different type called italics. If you were to ask your student to hand-copy this passage of the poem, would she know what to do when she came to the italicized word? (She would underline the name of the ship: <u>Somerset</u>.)

Language Arts: Poet - Henry Wadsworth Longfellow (1807-1882)

(**Teacher's Information**: Henry Wadsworth Longfellow was a popular American poet of the 1800s. Many of his works are still read and loved today. Longfellow wrote a long narrative poem called "Evangeline," and another called "The Song of Hiawatha," of which a small portion is well-known. If you enjoy Longfellow's poetry, find "The Children's Hour," which shows Longfellow's love of family life, and "The Village Blacksmith," which tells a "strong" story. Longfellow entered college at the age of fifteen, and had the future writer Nathaniel Hawthorne for a classmate. If you find a volume of collected works of Longfellow, you might find additional poems that you would enjoy.)

Language Arts: Vocabulary

(**Teacher's Note**: There are *lots* of new vocabulary words in this story, but *please* don't try to teach them all to your student. Just pick a few that are interesting to you.)

minutemen Members of the American militia, just before the Revolutionary War, who were ready to respond quickly.

weathercock A weathervane which turns with the wind and points the wind's direction.

belfry A bell tower.

spectral Like a phantom or ghostly appearance.

muffle (d) To deaden sound; In this story, cloth was wrapped around the oar locks to quiet (or muffle) the squeak of the oars.

moorings The cables by which a ship is tied; it can also be the post or dock where the boat is tied.

phantom A ghost.

magnify (ied) Make larger.

barrack A building or group of buildings used to house soldiers.

grenadiers A special British military unit of men.

stealthy Secret or sly.

sentinel A sentry or watch guard posted to watch and warn of danger.

impatient Not cheerfully willing to wait; wanting to get on with action.

impetuous Quick, rash or impulsive movement.

girth The band of a saddle that goes underneath the horse's belly.

somber Grave expression, without any humor.

steed Horse.

alders Type of tree which grows well near water.

gild (ed) Golden-colored (can be overlaid with actual gold or just made to look bright).

musket ball The lead ball fired from a musket, as a shell is fired from a shotgun or a bullet from a rifle.

British Regular Members of the standing British army.

defy (iance) To go against authority.

peril Something that may cause harm or injury.

hulk An abandoned ship; also a large person or object.

muster To assemble or summon troops, for inspection, roll call or service.

Art: Light as a Main Theme

Ask your student what is the exciting moment for which Paul Revere is waiting, saddled to ride. (He is waiting for a signal light, "one, if by land and two, if by sea.") Because the story pivots around a light, the artist has chosen to make light the main topic in each of the pictures. Lights in the houses, lights streaming through the open doorways, the light of the moon and its reflections. Light carries as a major theme throughout the illustrations of the story. Paul Revere, himself, and the other men who ride that night "en-**light**en" or bring awareness to the minutemen.

For your young student, you might just ask about the signal light and mention that the artist seemed to think light was important in the story. Let her leaf through the pictures, looking for examples of light.

Art: Use of Light and Contrast for Dramatic Effect

Ask your student to look at the pictures and name as many **sources** for the light in the paintings as she can. (She could name candles, moon, oil lamps from the houses, the lamps in the church tower, etc.)

The light on faces and scenery is in sharp contrast to the night dark. Ted Rand has used the effect of bright light on a dark night to paint a dramatic, exciting portrayal of a dramatic and exciting event.

Another famous children's poem is "Silver" by Walter de LaMare (1873-1956). "Silver" is a splendid poem that describes how moonlight changes everything in its path, including the paws of the dog and the fish in the stream:

"Slowly, silently, now the moon
Walks the night in her silver shoon ..." (shoes)

De LaMare's poem is rich in alliteration (the "s" sounds predominating) and is well worth finding and reading out loud several times. Any one of the lines of "Silver" would be excellent for your student to illustrate (emphasizing the use of light) or you may choose to illustrate some of *Paul Revere's Ride,* or both!

Art: Architecture - Colonial

By the time Paul Revere made his famous ride, the American colonies had grown from the rough beginnings of Plymouth and Jamestown to fashionable cities such as Boston. The architecture depicted in the story shows examples of the kinds of building and details of this colonial period.

Included in the illustrations to *Paul Revere's Ride* are white clapboard homes and buildings, two-story and brick homes (built with symmetry; count the windows on each side of the door and notice the balance). Many have neat, white picket fences, and brick chimneys (sometimes one on each side of the house, like the cover painting that you see when you unfold the hardcover book's jacket and spread it out.)

The white house with black shutters opposite the crowing rooster illustration, shows a pointed triangle over the door; this is called a **pediment**. (PED-uh-ment). Your student can find this type of architectural trim on many homes and buildings around her town. Also, the picture that goes with the pigeons and the line "Then he climbed to the tower of the Old North Church...", shows a tall window with a rounded top. This is called a palladian window. (puh-LAY-dee-un). These styles were popular in England at the time of Revere's ride (and brought to the colonies), and show classical Greek and Roman influence. Your student may also see examples of **palladian** windows as she looks at the homes and buildings around her even today.

Teacher's Note: The reason these styles are mentioned is not because there is a necessity for young children to memorize this information, but rather to enrich your student's awareness of the things around her. This allows her the excitement of finding things by her own observation that she's heard about in her lessons. Look for these architectural details in the pictures of your story and whenever you're on an outing:

Pediment   **Palladian Window**

Rose Window   **Doric Door**

If your student enjoyed this introduction to colonial architecture, also see the activity sheet at the end of this unit

Art: Reflections in Water

Opposite the third page of poetry in *Paul Revere's Ride*, you see a British man-of-war ship with a "double large" hulk, due to reflection in the water:

"And a huge black hulk, that was magnified
By its own reflection in the tide."

Show your young student the actual bottom of the ship where it meets the water, by running your finger under the boat. Explain the rest of the darkness is only a reflection of the hulk. See how it looks larger because of the reflection? You can also see the masts and the moon reflected in the water. Ask your older student why the reflections are wavy and separated into pieces. The moon is certainly not round in the water. (These are the artist's methods of portraying moving water. Perhaps the wind is blowing over the surface making waves. At any rate, the water is rippling and therefore the reflections are not perfect.)

Contrast this picture with the wonderful upside-down reflection of brave Paul Revere as he passes by the Mystic River. This picture is like a stop-action photograph, and the reflection must be on extremely calm and tranquil water because its image is not broken up. Even the moon looks more rounded.

Find a pond or lake near you and point out reflections of objects in the calm waters and in moving water. Notice the differences. If you are able, wait for a night with a full moon and watch its reflection on the water. Talk about what you see and try capturing what you see on paper.

Also, opposite the page from the gravestones you can see the long broken ribbon of moonlight on the water. Your older student might be able to comprehend that this long ribbon of light is caused by the angle of the moon being lower on the horizon, rather than directly overhead. Perhaps some experiments with a flashlight in a darkened room would help increase the understanding of light and the angles from which it can come.

Math: Subtracting Dates - Solving a Riddle

In the beginning of his poem, Henry Wadsworth Longfellow writes: "Hardly a man is now alive who remembers that famous day and year." Ask your older student if she knows what is meant by this line or if she can figure it out. (The "famous day and year" is April 18, 1775. Longfellow wrote the poem in the year 1861. At that time, anyone who had been alive on April 18, 1775, would have been 86 years old. Eighty-six was an extremely old age for the time period of the 1800s. So Longfellow writes, "Hardly a man is now alive who remembers ..."To solve the riddle, you have to know that the poem was written in 1861.)

Try subtracting other dates such as: if you [the teacher] were born in [year], how old were you when your student was born in [year]?, etc. Make up problems using family members, pets, relatives, etc.

Science: Fog Over Rivers

Fog is formed by evaporated water moisture from lakes, oceans and rivers. Very moist soil or plants can also cause evaporation that results in fog. In *Paul Revere's Ride* the rider " ... felt the damp of the river fog, that rises after the sun goes down." Fog rises after the sun goes down because the temperature of the air drops. This cools and condenses the water vapor into the tiny droplets of fog. Fog disappears when the temperature rises. The air can once again hold more of the uncondensed water vapor. Any time you have an evening outing, look for fog over water areas and point it out to your student. (If she doesn't show you first!) Remind your student that you can see your breath in cold weather. This phenomenon is caused by the moist air which you exhale condensing upon contact with the cold outside air and causing "fog!"

Teacher's Notes

The *Five in a Row* lesson options for each unit in the manual are all you need to teach your child. The additional resource area provided below is simply a place to jot down relevant info you've found that you might want to reference.

PAUL REVERE'S RIDE

Date:

Student:

70

Five in a Row Lesson Topics Chosen:

Social Studies:

Language Arts:

Art:

Math:

Science:

Relevant Library Resources:
Books, DVDs, Audio Books

Websites or Video Links:

Related Field Trip Opportunities:

Favorite Quote or Memory During Study:

Name:

Date:

Art: **Architecture - Colonial**

Monticello, Virginia

Like Paul Revere, Thomas Jefferson played an important part in the early history of the United States. Among his contributions, Jefferson helped write the Declaration of Independence. He lived his later years in a home which he designed and built, called Monticello, which means "little mountain." Look at the picture and see if you and your student can find examples of:

Pediment

Palladian Window

Rose Window

Doric Door

Every year many people visit Monticello (located in Virginia) and enjoy the architecture, gardens and artistic creativity of Thomas Jefferson. Perhaps someday you'll have a chance to visit, too!

After reading the lesson and brainstorming ideas of secret communication methods, ask your older student to invent their own secret communication method to tell you or a sibling something.

*One example could be: a certain pattern of LEGO® bricks representing a word or action.

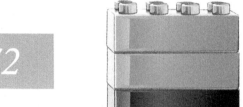

— Yellow

— Yellow

— Green

This Means Stop

— Green

— Green

— Yellow

This Means Go

Name:

Date:

Language Arts: **Vocabulary**

Charades Game

Copy this page then cut out and shuffle the action vocabulary words.
Have your student pick one to act out. Your student can also add more
action words to the back of the cards.

It's a good idea to laminate the page before cutting out the cards, to make them more durable.

Muffle	**Magnify**	**Stealthy**
Impatient	**Somber**	**Impetuous**
Sentinel	**Steed**	**Muster**

Henry The Castaway

Title:	*Henry The Castaway*
Author:	Mark Taylor
Illustrator:	Graham Booth
Copyright:	1972
Award:	Junior Literary Guild Selection
Summary:	Henry loves exploring expeditions, big words and being rescued!

Social Studies: Explorers

Explorers are people who have an excitement in their hearts about seeing places that have been considered remote or unknown. Explorers are usually different from pioneers, because they would rather discover than begin to live in the land they find. Explorers are often considered courageous because they face many dangers being in unknown (at least to them) territory. Explorers make use of any maps that exist of the area they are seeking, and often make new maps once they have been there. They sometimes carry flags to claim the new territories they find.

Ask your student if he thinks Henry had the true heart of an explorer based on the above criteria.

You can plan explorations with your student of unknown areas, including the back woods, a new park or your city. (Try finding all the interesting places.) If your student is interested, help him plan and explore a new area and see if he has the heart of an explorer. Remember, not everyone is an explorer. Some are pioneers, helping to develop new territories but moving on when an area becomes too civilized. Some are settlers, coming to live and stay and build. (Even today, whether we are talking about cities, businesses or families, there are some people who are the explorer, pioneer or settler types.) There is a blessing in the fact that all types of people are needed; explorers are only one type.

Have your student place the story disk wherever *he* would like to explore, since no actual location is given in the story.

Language Arts: Vocabulary

Orinoco River (OHR-uh-NOH-koh) a river in South America, 2,384 miles long, forming the boundary between Colombia and Venezuela.

crocodiles A reptile with short legs, a long, low, thick body and long powerful tail. Crocodiles live in tropical countries in swampy areas, mostly in the Eastern Hemisphere, but four species live in North and South America. North America is also home to the alligator, a similar reptile.

yellow fever A viral disease transmitted by mosquitoes. It affects the liver and, therefore, victims often have a yellow pigmentation to their skin. Once common in Central America, parts of South America and Africa, it has now been controlled by mosquito netting, repellent and insecticides. There is also a vaccine that can protect against yellow fever.

Language Arts: Literary Device - Allusion

An allusion is a reference in literature to a well known or familiar person, place, thing or event. The allusion is used to give more description and information. To use the phrase, "he had the Midas touch," one needs to know about King Midas and his story, or the allusion goes unnoticed. There are allusions to famous literary figures and historic figures within *Henry The Castaway*, and you may or may not feel it necessary to point these out and explain:

When Henry landed on the island and found friendly natives, he named the cat Mrs. Friday. This is an allusion to the famous story of *Robinson Crusoe* (which Henry had obviously read). Robinson Crusoe was a castaway on an island and found a native who he named Friday.

Henry names the kittens Columbus and Elizabeth, references to the man who discovered the New World, and a queen during whose reign England ruled the seas.

Perhaps your older student would enjoy reading *Robinson Crusoe* by Daniel Defoe, or he may like to write an adventure story of his own using a few allusions to famous persons, places, things or events. There are several abridged, illustrated versions of Robinson Crusoe available at different reading levels or for read-aloud time. You may also enjoy similar editions of *Treasure Island* and *Kidnapped* by Robert Louis Stevenson. All manner of fun could result from readings such as these: treasure hunts and boat rides and adventurous expeditions—all filled with imagination!

Language Arts: Drama

This story would make a fine short play. Your young student might enjoy taking on the role of Henry. You could help him make flags (for marking his trail and for claiming new lands), and designate different parts of the room as the different areas of the story. Help him find a box or something to use for a canoe, and maybe some stuffed animals for the friendly natives. He would probably like to make a shelter from two chairs and a blanket, and enjoy using a real flashlight.

Again, the lines could be kept to a minimum with you or an older student narrating most of the story.

If your student enjoys acting before an audience, invite family or friends to see your production. If he is hesitant, have loads of fun just pretending together!

Art: Expressions

The expressions on the faces of the characters are interesting. Notice Henry's expressions and how they change. Look, too, at the cat and kittens. Begin where Henry finds the "friendly natives" and look carefully at each situation in which they appear and the accompanying expressions on their faces.

Art: Mixed Medium and Effects of Water

It looks like Graham Booth may have used more than one medium for these pictures of Henry's adventures. There are places that look like water color and others that look like marker, etc.

In many of the illustrations, you can see how this artist chose to draw water. The cover pictures shows the lines streaming back behind the boat and in many places you see the broken circles around an object in the water.

Math: Counting and Tallying

After you have read the book for the day, go back and let your student hunt for animals in the illustrations, even the hidden ones (there is one hawk that is very difficult to spot!). There are many animals and birds throughout the pictures. As your student finds each one, have him make a vertical mark on a piece of paper. When he has found five, have him make the fifth mark diagonally across the four previous vertical marks for a tally. When he is finished, teach him to count by fives to see how many animals he was able to find. By doing this exercise, he will begin to learn for himself how helpful the tally method is for counting and how quickly one can count by fives. (**Teacher's Note:** You need to decide if your student is ready for this lesson. Tallying may be fun for your student even if the counting by fives comes later.)

Science: Survival Skills

Henry practices many good survival skills in his busy life of exploring the world around him. Can your student name some of them? (He takes many flags to mark his path and to let others know where he has been. He has carefully left these flags upstream and he also thinks to send his floating signals down the river. He takes food and other supplies along with him. He carries a working flashlight and has a companion dog to share his adventures—he doesn't go alone. He *notices* that the storm is coming up and wisely builds a shelter. Then, he uses his flashlight and his dog's barking to help notify rescuers.)

Henry also knows that to get a better view, it helps if you are higher up, and so he climbs a tree. Good survival skills include the knowledge that a tree, tall rock, etc., can be used to gain a better view. (Remember *Harold and the Purple Crayon* by Crockett Johnson in FIAR Vol. 2? He drew a mountain to climb so he could gain a better view.)

Science: River Current

Rivers have a **source** (where the water begins to flow) and a **mouth** (the place where the river spills into a lake, larger river, ocean or sea). When a person stands on the banks of a river, the water is flowing in a particular direction from its source to its mouth. This direction determines the river's current. **Upstream** is toward the source of the river (where it begins), and **downstream** means toward the mouth of the river (where the river ends). **Current** always flows downstream.

Henry gets into the canoe and drifts naturally downstream on the current. He realizes that upstream there were flags to show that he had been there. However, he decides to put some flags on sticks and let them follow the current downstream to be doubly sure he is rescued. Discuss Henry's wisdom in sending signal flags downstream and the fact that Henry knows about river currents.

A. A. Milne wrote a story that would go well with this lesson on currents. In *The House At Pooh Corner*, there is a chapter called "In Which Pooh Invents a New Game and Eeyore Joins In." Pooh, in this chapter, throws a pine cone over one side of the bridge. He then notices that pine cone coming out under the bridge on the other side moving downstream with the current. He wonders if this will happen every time and does some experiments. He discovers that it does. Eventually, he makes a game with his friends. He uses sticks because they're easier to mark than pinecones. They throw two or more sticks in the water on one side of the bridge and then wait to see whose stick comes under the bridge first. There is more excitement when Eeyore comes floating down the current and a rescue is made! A great read-aloud anytime.

Science: Birds - Kingfisher

The title page shows Henry and Laird Angus McAngus drifting down the river current in a canoe. Ask your student to point out the creature that is watching them. Can he identify this bird? It is called a kingfisher. These birds have large heads and long bills. In the United States, we have the belted kingfisher which spends much time on tree limbs watching over streams for small fish. When he sees a fish, he dives for it. Kingfishers also sometimes eat crayfish, frogs, insects and other small water life. If you have a river, pond or stream nearby, look for kingfishers on tree branches or stumps. They can be seen in most of the United States but they are scarce in the New England area. Look for a short video online or a children's book at the library that includes the belted kingfisher.

Science: Dog Breeds - Scottish Terrier

Laird Angus McAngus is a Scottish name.* The author chose this name for Henry's dog because it is a Scottish Terrier. This breed of dogs was first raised in the highlands of Scotland. Its common nickname is a Scottie. The name **terrier** comes from the Latin word terra or earth because these dogs were used to drive game out of their holes or homes in the ground. Look online or in a dog breed book from the library for photographs of the Scottish Terrier. Your student may have never seen a Scottish Terrier in real life and will enjoy seeing actual photos of the same dog that is in his picture book!

*Your student may remember that the boy nicknamed Wee Gillis (FIAR Vol. 2) who lived in Scotland, had an unusually long Scottish name: Alastair Roderic Craigellachie Dalhousie Gowan Donnybristle MacMac. Again, this name as well as Laird Angus McAngus, are only pointed out so your student will have a chance to enjoy the "sounds" of Scotland. Perhaps in the future he will recognize Scottish-sounding names as an enjoyable enrichment to his world.

Teacher's Note: If your student likes Henry and Angus, there are three more books in this series, each tied to season of the year: *Henry the Explorer*, *Henry Explores the Jungle*, and *Henry Explores the Mountains*.

Teacher's Notes

The *Five in a Row* lesson options for each unit in the manual are all you need to teach your child. The additional resource area provided below is simply a place to jot down relevant info you've found that you might want to reference.

HENRY THE CASTAWAY

Date: _____

Student: _____

Five in a Row Lesson Topics Chosen:

Social Studies: _____
_____
_____

Language Arts: _____
_____
_____

Art: _____
_____
_____

Math: _____
_____
_____

Science: _____
_____
_____

Relevant Library Resources: Books, DVDs, Audio Books
_____
_____
_____
_____
_____
_____

Websites or Video Links:
_____
_____
_____
_____
_____
_____
_____
_____

Related Field Trip Opportunities:
_____
_____
_____

Favorite Quote or Memory During Study:
_____
_____
_____

Name:

Date:

Math: **Counting and Tallying**

After you have read the book for the day, go back and let your student hunt for animals in the illustrations, even the hidden ones (there is one hawk that is very difficult to spot!). There are many animals and birds throughout the pictures. As your student finds each one, have him make a vertical mark on a piece of paper. When he has found five, have him make the fifth mark diagonally across the four previous vertical marks for a tally.

Example:

List animals found:

_____

_____

_____

_____

_____

_____

_____

Tally marks:

Total

Name:

Date:

Science: **Survival Skills**

Henry practices many good survival skills in his busy life of exploring the world around him. Can your student name some of them?

List of items Henry took:

_____

_____

_____

_____

_____

_____

Create a survival checklist for items you would take on an exploration:

_____

_____

_____

_____

_____

Name:

Date:

Social Studies: **Exploration**

As an optional go-along activity, get the book *Seaman's Journal: On the Trail with Lewis and Clark* by Patricia Reeder Eubank from the library. Read it with your student one or more times. Keep a list of things the the explorers prepared and used on their journey. Write them into the appropriate categories below.

Items/Tools	Food	Misc.
_____	_____	_____
_____	_____	_____
_____	_____	_____
_____	_____	_____
_____	_____	_____
_____	_____	_____
_____	_____	_____
_____	_____	_____
_____	_____	_____
_____	_____	_____
_____	_____	_____
_____	_____	_____

The Finest Horse in Town

Title:	*The Finest Horse in Town*
Author:	Jacqueline Briggs Martin
Illustrator:	Susan Gaber
Copyright:	1992
Summary:	A horse, three stories and a summertime of entertainment and possibilities.

Social Studies: Geography and Time Setting

The story of *The Finest Horse in Town* takes place in Maine, one of the New England states on the Atlantic coast of the eastern United States. The information on the book jacket and the illustrations place the time of the story at the turn of the century. You might talk over with your student what the phrase "turn of the century" means. Which turn of the century does this book refer to? Which one occurred after that?

The story also covers the Fourth of July. You could take this opportunity to discuss the beginning of the United States of America at any level you choose. Notice the Fourth of July celebration in the illustrations. There are many flags and streamers, and Sandman even has red, white and blue suspenders! The sisters buy lemons and ice and everyone has lemonade. Talk with your student about special ways of celebrating this holiday. Maybe she will think of some new traditions like a red, white and blue cake, reading poems of "Paul Revere's Ride" by Longfellow, the "Concord Hymn" by Ralph Waldo Emerson, singing patriotic songs or having other special events of the day to mark the birthday of the United States. Place your story disk on Maine.

Social Studies: Relationships - Difficult People and Stealing

In the character of Hooks the trader, you have opportunity to discuss the subject of dishonesty. If Prince belonged to your student, how would she feel about Hooks and his lying, stealing and trickery? What do the sisters do? Would your student react in the same way they did? (Stella worries the most and is rather pessimistic. Cora is quiet and careful and more practical in her reply. They both tell all their friends and soon the whole village is watching for the horse. The good neighbors who find the horse provide a contrast to the treachery of Hooks.)

(**Teacher's Note:** Using your own judgment for age appropriateness, you might decide to mention the treatment of Hooks as a stereotypical character. In many books, plays, shows and movies, the "horse trader" is characterized as unscrupulous or shrewd. Whereas your student is learning to discern each person by their works, it may increase her understanding of the things she reads and sees to know that Hooks is a general **stereotyped character.**)

Hooks is eventually found out. Ask your student how Hooks responds and what happens to him. People who act in an unscrupulous way have to be moving on because no one trusts them or wants to be friends with them unless they change their unsociable behavior.

Social Studies: Relationships - Gratefulness

In each of the story scenarios, the sisters give presents to those who help them. Ask your student to listen for the gifts and match them to the particular story. (Old Hartford receives a pair of their best work shoes and a bell for the newborn calf. They give Sandman a new silver harmonica and a fat rooster. The girl gets a winter coat from Boston and her brother receives a fur hat.) This would also be a good project for an art picture. Your student could draw each character with their corresponding gift. Discuss with your student that we sometimes express our gratitude with gifts. Other times just a simple "thank you" is enough. But having a grateful heart and expressing our gratitude to others is important. What kind of things has your student done lately to tell or show someone her gratitude?

Language Arts: Reminiscing

"Long before my mother was born, her aunts owned a store ..." begins the story. This type of story beginning, of looking back into the past by personal experience is called **reminiscing**. With your young student you could just point out that the author chose to tell her story from a memory (and several suppositions) of long ago. This is only one kind of beginning that a story might have. Have your student find out some things that happened long before her parents were born and talk about them. If your young student is excited about the project, let her dictate a story to you about what happened long before her mother, brother, etc. was born. Then, let her illustrate her story.

With your older student, you might want to talk about the word "reminiscing" and then do any of the projects listed above. Remind her to be looking for other stories that begin in this way. Add "Reminiscing" to Story Beginnings in your list of Choices a Writer Can Make.

Language Arts: Stories Inside Stories

Jacqueline Briggs Martin has written a story that has three additional stories inside of it. This approach uses lots of characters and scenarios. If your student enjoys diagramming a story, you might try taking a chart-sized piece of paper (or three pages of paper) and outlining the details of each of the "perhaps" stories. It could look something like this:

Hooks

• Keeps Prince in barn

• Brings Prince at 5 o'clock on Wednesdays

• Has a sharp eye, knows Prince is valuable

• Tries to convince the aunts to sell

• Paints spots on Prince with shoe polish

• Hides him in a back pasture

• Is found out and has to leave town

Sandman Bonney

• Loses a leg in a logging accident

• Loves horses

• Plays harmonica

• He loves a good joke, like the turtle that needs suspenders

• Surprises sisters with Fourth of July dancing Prince

• Receives a silver harmonica and a fat rooster

• Teaches the rooster to dance

The Children

• Brother and sister

• Father a farmer and mother sews

• Children get two pennies a week to watch Prince

• Feed him carrots and apples, and water

• They have to watch for breaks in the wall and find Prince if he gets lost

• Nurse him through his sickness (many details ...)

• Receive a coat and hat

The writing technique of "stories within stories" is probably too advanced for your young student, but your older student may want to try such a writing adventure. If she does, be encouraging and remember to add "Stories Within Stories" to your list of Choices a Writer Can Make.

Art: Recognizing Watercolor

Turn with your student to p. 25 and see if she can name the art medium Susan Gaber used to paint the barn or house. (Watercolor is easily recognized in this picture by the watery splotches and the light, translucent, see-through quality of the paint.) Look together for other evidence of watercolor splotches and see-through quality. Your student will soon be able to tell the difference between a watercolor painting, an oil, tempera, colored pencils or pastels, etc. Using only one or two colors on wet paper, let your student try to achieve the splotchy effect. If the design is pleasing, use it for a make-your-own book cover for any of your student's stories.

Art: Illustrating the Parade

Let your student recite a list of the people that followed Prince and the sisters in the big parade. She could choose anyone from the list to illustrate: The grocer on his float, the fire wagon, hay wagon, etc. If she is going to use watercolor for her illustrations, remind her that she probably should pencil sketch her ideas lightly before she begins to paint. Then, after the watercolor is dry, she can gently erase the lines if she wishes.

Art: Noticing the Details

Remember to look for shadows, reflections and turtle tracks. And encourage your student if she points them out to you first!

Look through the illustrations to see the expressions on the faces of the different characters and even the animals. Notice the action in the figures, how the arms, hands and legs show movement in both the people and animals. Look for each of these groups of details one at a time, looking for just body action through the story, and then the expressions through the story, etc.

Susan Gaber, the illustrator, has painted different dresses for the sisters. Notice the poppy skirt in the poppy field, and appreciate with your student the realism of different clothes for the different days.

Looking at pp. 30-31 of your story (the picnic scene), ask your student which trees are old trees and which ones are younger trees. Enjoy together the fact that this artist uses variety. Notice that some of trees are green (like evergreens) and some have turned fall colors (like maples, oaks, birches, aspens, etc.) Again, Gaber uses variety in her work, and you can add "Variety" to the list of Choices an Artist Can Make to help remind your student of good compositional ideas.

The story opens with a watch face, and then p. 32 shows a watch closed. Ask your student why she thinks this is. (It seems to be a symbolic way of saying, "The End.")

Art: Backgrounds

Pages 16 and 17 show Graber's choice of technique for background that uses three horizontal strips of color. There is a thin blue strip in the foreground for the water, a thin brown strip for the sand or dirt and a wide chartreuse strip for the grass or meadow. Your student could vary the type of strips (like path, woods and sky; or plains, hills and mountains) and use torn colored paper strips to make a background for a picture. (She could also use watercolor.) Then draw or print out pictures of people, buildings, cars, animals, etc. to paste over the background to finish the work.

(Although the author used three strips of color, your student can use as many or as few as she wishes. She could simply use a blue strip for sky and a brown strip for the ground. But she could also use a dozen strips with several diferent colors for the sky at sunset, several colors for the grays and purples of distant mountain ranges and several strips for the roads and fields of the foreground, for instance.)

Art: Overlapping, a Function of Perspective

The bowl of round candy balls on p. 22 is a good example of overlapping objects. To try this principle, set a bowl piled high with apples in front of your student and talk about the fact that you can probably see the entire outline of only one of the apples. Just a portion of the outline of the others is visible because they are behind the one on top, etc.

An artist who attempts to draw what she actually sees, uses overlapping to give the effect of some items being behind others. Look on p. 21 at the lemons, and on p. 23 at the candy jar. In the candy jar the scoop has the top candy ball and the rest are overlapping one

another. Ask your student, after looking at her bowl of apples, which bowl below looks more realistic (like the real apples).

Your young student will benefit from just an introduction to this concept and looking at the real apples and the pictures of the lemons and candy. Your older student may want to try a few exercises in overlapping and begin noticing this technique in other works of art and illustrations.

There are excellent lessons in overlapping in Dan O'Neill's *The Big Yellow Drawing Book* and in Bruce McIntyre's *Drawing Textbook*.

Art: Seeing Artwork in Many Proportions

Children are often "patterned" to see art work in 8 1/2 x 11 inch proportions because that is the size of the paper they are most often given for a project. The picture on p. 25 (with the cat and the large tree) shows an illustration almost three times as wide as it is high. Let your student see the picture and talk about how wide it is. Does your student think it looks unusual? Does she like it? Throughout the next few weeks, try giving her different sized pieces of paper and letting her think what kinds of subjects would go well on paper of that proportion. Or use 8 1/2 x 11 inch paper and draw large shapes such as circles, triangles, squares or rectangles and then ask your student to draw her picture *inside* the shapes. Perhaps each different shape of working area will inspire a certain special subject for her composition.

Then, if you can, take your student to an art gallery and enjoy looking at the different works of art. See if she notices pictures of unusual proportion; very narrow canvases or even a round picture. This can be a discovery tour rather than lecture.

Art: Drawing a Moving Flag

Have your student examine the flag on the book's cover. When the wind blows a flag, it "ripples," allowing only a portion to be seen at any one time. As a simple "help" to draw a wind-blown flag, try holding two pencils simultaneously and drawing parallel, wiggly lines and then connect the vertical segments as shown below. You'll have to erase several small portions of curves which should not show as noted below. Now let your student try this fun way to draw flags.

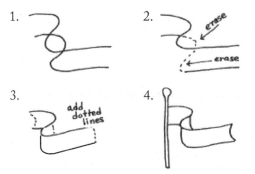

For more advanced techniques in flag drawing, see Bruce McIntyre's *Drawing Textbook*. Great directions!

Math: Century and Counting by Hundreds

The word century comes from the Latin and means one hundred. Remind your student that a century covers one hundred years. For your older student, name a few past events and let her figure out how many centuries have passed since they occurred.

Counting by hundreds is considered by some to be a second grade skill. If your student is ready, introduce counting by hundreds. Remember that the sisters in this story ran a store. Ask your student if each dollar is the same as a hundred pennies, how many dollars would the sisters have if a customer paid them with one, two, three, four, or five hundred pennies?

Math: Multiplying by Twos

When the children watch Prince, they receive two pennies each week. Using the enjoyable scenario of the children's wages, explore the subject of multiplying by twos. For your young student, talk about the children being paid two pennies a week and put two pennies on the table. Let her make a tally mark for one week. Then put out two more pennies and she will mark another week, etc. Let her count the marks (for example, three) and then count all the pennies (six). Two each week for three weeks is six pennies or six cents. 2 x 3 = 6. Let this just be a fun introduction to multiplication.

For your older student, use the scenario to actually teach the twos tables. You may still use pennies to illustrate. Two pennies for 1, 2, 3, 4, 5, etc. weeks.

For your oldest student, talk about the amount of the wages and the value of a penny at the turn of the century. Also, how much would the children earn in 25 weeks? 52 weeks?

Math: Telling Time

The Finest Horse In Town begins with a watch and shows a watch on several pages: 4, 6, 7, 14, 23, and 32. The artist and author obviously portrayed time and the telling of time as significant. You may wish to use this opportunity to inspire your young student. For

instance: Did you see the watch at the beginning of the story? Let's look for other watches. Why do you think there are so many pictures of telling time? Is it important for a shopkeeper to know how to tell time? (What time do they open in the morning? When do they close?)

Your student could make a list of ways to tell time: the sun itself or sundials, hour glasses and minute timers, watches, pocket watches, grandfather clocks, cuckoo clocks, digital clocks, stop watches, smartphones, etc.

You could also make a list of occupations where timing is an important part of the job: the transportation industry that has to run on schedule; medical personnel that have to dispense medicine on time; the radio and television broadcasting industry that runs on a daily schedule; any type of food production where baking, cooking times are important, etc. This list will grow as you add new occupations whenever they occur to you.

Now try a list of things your student has to time in a day. How often does she say, "Is it time for … ?" Let your older student practice telling time on watches, stop watches and clocks (analog and digital). If your older student is extremely interested in the topic of time, you could introduce the topics of Greenwich Mean Time, the time zones of the United States, the International Dateline or military time.

Begin a list of phrases with the word time in them: old time, summertime, on time, in time, for all time, time-in or time-out, time's up, a stitch in time, time zone, daylight savings time, time's a wastin', timekeeper, Father Time, by the time, timeless, it's about time, time limit, time exposure, time and a half, etc. Keep this list in a notebook, bring it out "from time to time" and add to it! This type of list-making is great fun while traveling by bus or car.

Science: Caring for Horses

Remind your student that after all the dancing and hoopla of the Fourth of July parade, Prince is quietly munching his oats. Ask your student what horses eat. What does Prince eat in this story? (Oats, carrots, apples, treats, and the chokecherries that made him sick.) What are other things horses eat? (Grass, well-cured hay, alfalfa, sweet feed which is a variety of grain: oat, millet, corn, wheat and barley, all slightly moistened with black strap molasses. Also minerals, salt, and good water.) There are many types of plants that can make a horse sick like the chokecherries, so a good horse owner is careful about where her horse grazes. Horses also need shelter, grooming (especially checking their feet and legs), exercise and love. Remember: Good people are kind to their animals.

Science: Ice from the Ice House

At the Fourth of July celebration, the sisters order blocks of ice and lemons, and lemonade is served to everyone. At the turn of the century, much of the ice used by the public was still cut from frozen lakes and kept all summer, packed in sawdust in ice houses. These businesses sold the blocks of ice to the people to keep their food cool in iceboxes, and to make things like lemonade and ice cream. The ice chips the children receive from Pettengill's Ice House on the Fourth of July are a special treat!

Science: Trees and Fall Colors

The red and orange trees at the end of the third portion of the story show the fall season. If appropriate, you may want to introduce or review why some trees turn beautiful colors in the fall. A simplified explanation is that with the cooler weather and the reduction of hours of daylight, the chemical processes of the leaves begin to shut down. Chlorophyll (the substance that makes the leaves green) breaks down and the colors in the leaves that have been overshadowed by the green, are now visible. Different types of trees have different colored leaves in the fall. Some oak and maple trees have red leaves while other maples have orange leaves. Some aspen, elm, maple, and birch have yellow leaves. Look together at a reference book for some examples of bright fall color.

Teacher's Notes

The *Five in a Row* lesson options for each unit in the manual are all you need to teach your child. The additional resource area provided below is simply a place to jot down relevant info you've found that you might want to reference.

THE FINEST HORSE IN TOWN

Date: _____

Student: _____

Five in a Row Lesson Topics Chosen:

Social Studies:
_____
_____
_____

Language Arts:
_____
_____
_____

Art:
_____
_____
_____

Math:
_____
_____
_____

Science:
_____
_____

Relevant Library Resources: Books, DVDs, Audio Books

_____
_____
_____
_____
_____
_____
_____

Websites or Video Links:

_____
_____
_____
_____
_____
_____
_____
_____

Related Field Trip Opportunities:
_____
_____
_____

Favorite Quote or Memory During Study:
_____
_____
_____

92

Name:

Date:

Art: **Seeing Artwork in Many Proportions**

Children are often "patterned" to see art work in 8 1/2 x 11 inch proportions because that is the size of the paper they are most often given for a project.

Try drawing a picture inside the different shapes/sizes below.

Name:

Date:

Geography: **Maine Flag**

The flag of Maine has a blue field with Maine's state coat of arms at the center. The state's coat of arms depicts a moose resting under a tall pine tree, a farmer and a seaman showing the state's reliance on agriculture and the sea, and the North Star representing the state motto: "dirigo" which means "I Lead." *For more information, see Parts of a Flag on page 224.*

Color in the Maine flag below.

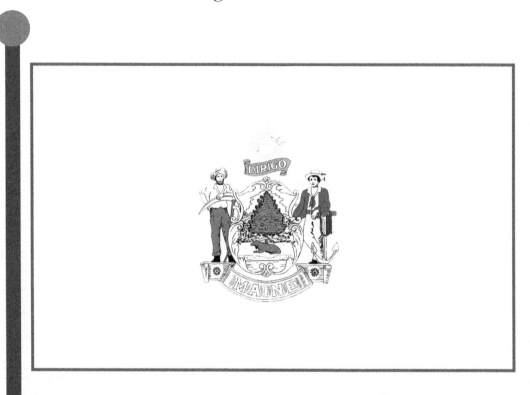

Name:

Date:

Math: **Telling Time**

Familiarize your young student with the face of a clock. Have them write in the numbers around the clock face.

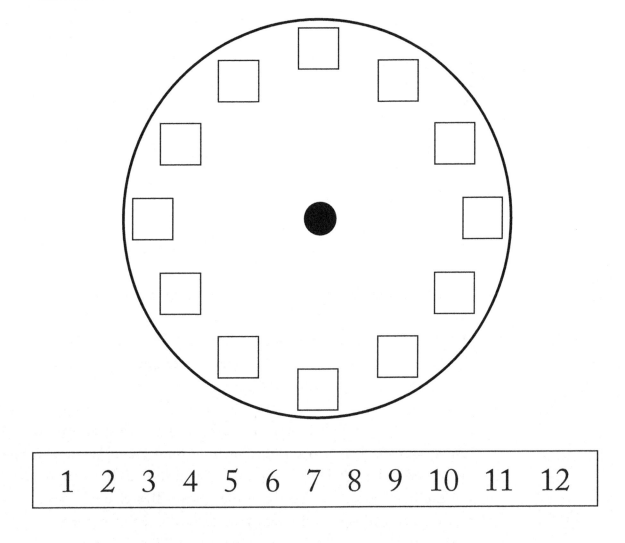

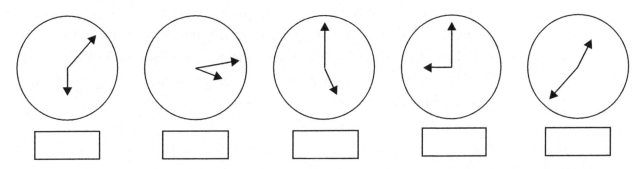

1   2   3   4   5   6   7   8   9   10   11   12

For an older student have them fill in the correct time on each clock below.

Truman's Aunt Farm

Title: *Truman's Aunt Farm*
Author: Jama Kim Rattigan
Illustrator: G. Brian Karas
Copyright: 1994
Summary: A longed-for birthday present turns into a "relative project."

Social Studies: Relationships - Character Traits

(**Teacher's Note:** You may want to wait till later in the week for this exercise, after you have read through the book a number of times.)

Character is the way a person acts; the values by which he lives. Search the text of the story to find clues to Truman's character; what he was like. (Truman is *cautious* when he opens the box from Aunt Fran. He is *orderly* on the fourth and fifth page. His hat is on the peg, his pencils neatly in the holder, and the items are stored neatly in the basket. This character trait is continued when he inspects the aunt troops, devises a system for orderly food pick-up and sets a schedule of training events. Truman is *loving* and *wise* in his care of the aunts. He thinks about good food for them, helps them find the things at which they excel, helps them become more considerate and makes sure they get plenty of exercise and rest. Finally, he makes a plan to find children who will love them. (The aunt holding the balloon on the inside cover of the book jacket and the aunts that make the quilt on the back cover show that they love Truman, too.)

Social Studies: Relationships -Aunt

What is an aunt? Ask your student if he knows and if he has any aunts. Place the story disk where his aunt lives if he has one, or where he wishes an aunt might live.

In the story *Truman's Aunt Farm*, what is it that Truman finds out about having more than two hundred aunts? (That they weren't *his* aunts, and though they were great and all different, they were no substitute for his own Aunt Fran.)

Explore with your student the relationship of aunt. You may want to include anyone acting in the capacity of an aunt.

Anytime is a great time to write letters. The text with the letters and responses may inspire your student to write a letter to his own aunt! He can always add his own drawings in the margins or on separate paper.

Language Arts: Homophones

Homophones are words that sound alike but are spelled differently and have different meanings. The story *Truman's Aunt Farm* is based on a mix-up with the words **ant** and **aunt** which are **homophones**. Your young student may find this story funny, but your second through fourth grade student will fully appreciate the humor in the homophone mix-up. Some additional homophones are:

stair	stare
hair	hare
rain	reign, rein
stake	steak
bare	bear
two	to, too
pair	pear, pare
pray	prey
mail	male
plain	plane

Learning the differences in spelling and definition is considered by some to be third and fourth grade level skills. If your student can read and enjoys playing with words, you can make word games for him with homophones. The *Amelia Bedelia* books by Peggy Parish are based on mix-ups due to homophones (and homographs*) and are extremely humorous. These stories are a quick way to let your student understand the importance of communicating exactly what he means, and understanding that when other people say things, there may be more than one meaning to their words!

*Homographs** are words that are spelled the same but have different meanings: A "CON-vict" is someone in prison and to "con-VICT" is to influence someone that he's done wrong; "stalk" means both a stem of a plant and to pursue someone stealthily. In addition, **homonyms** are words that sound alike but have different meanings … and this is where the distinctions get very tricky and confusing even for adults! If you (the teacher) are interested, you could research these terms further, but for your student's purposes, "homophone" is a great place to start and end this lesson.

Language Arts: Perspective

Truman's Aunt Farm is told from the perspective of a young person. The reader is seeing all the events, and feeling all the feelings of this young person. How Truman views life and aunts and ants is what the reader learns. Truman goes about his business and solves his problems as he has seen adults doing, and with a great deal of order, wisdom and love. There probably isn't much to share with your student on this point. He needs to just enjoy the story, but this information is listed for the teacher.

Your older student may want to try a story with a similar theme including the mood of love and respect found in *Truman's Aunt Farm*. He may set forth a problem and try to solve it from a child's point of view, probably including humorous incidents.

Language Arts: Repetition

Ask your student if he noticed any repetitive lines in the story. (Near the beginning of the story, Truman reads the green card which says, "... free ants! Watch them work! Watch them play! Watch them eat! Live ants!" Much later in the book, Truman puts up a sign which repeats much of the former lines, "Live Aunts! Watch them work! Watch them play! Watch them eat!" There is also the repetition of the boxes arriving. The first box arrives. Truman cautiously looks at it, picks it up, turns it over and smells it. With the second box he repeats his actions, but the results are different.)

The author uses repetition to create balance and closure. What was begun has now ended.

Language Arts: Make a List of Activities

Look through the illustrations and list the activities in which you see the happy aunts participating. Later, when you read the story again, see if there are any activities in the text that you missed when making your list. Some activities include: playing badminton, looking for bird nests, painting, taking naps, etc.

Art: Use of Color to Enhance Mood and Create Unity

The bright spring greens of the cover are found consistently on every page of illustration. This provides a **unity** in the work. The spring green is a cheerful color, bursting with life. There is certainly life and action in every picture! In choosing the greens to illustrate the story, the artist has blended color with the **mood** of the text. Remind your student that if he illustrates a story, he can choose his "Colors to Agree with the Mood" of that story. Add this idea to your list of Choices an Artist Can Make.

Art: Techniques for Faces and Figures

G. Brian Karas, the illustrator, has used stylized figures with unusual techniques for faces and bodies. Ask your student to look at some of the figures and see if he can tell aspects of the bodies and faces that are different from many of the other types of illustrations he has seen. In other words, what makes Karas' figures unusual? (The hands and feet are very tiny, compared to the body. The faces have noses that are pointed and cheeks that are coiled circles or circles with lines. The eyes are either tiny dots when open or half circles with lash lines and the lips look like hearts with a line through them.) If your student would like, he may try some figures like Karas has made and maybe go on to invent some new looks all his own.

| Nose | Eyes | Cheeks | Mouth |

(Notice, too, the arm and leg action, especially in the illustration where the aunts are blowing bubbles and playing badminton on the lawn.)

Art: Humor in Illustrations

Look with your student at the title page. If he has ever had or seen a real plastic ant farm, he will appreciate the humor of this picture. Ask your student if he thinks the picture on p. 3 is humorous and why. (The ants are on tractors, with hoes and rakes, etc.) Look through the illustrations at the aunts' zany clothes. What makes these clothes seem humorous? (Notice their unusual color and pattern combinations.)

Math: Stamps and Postage

Since the story deals with sending and receiving letters and parcels by mail, this is a good time to explore postage. Show your student an envelope you've received in the mail that has a stamp. How much does it cost to mail a first class letter? If you have stamps at home, show them to your student. Explain why we need to affix postage to a letter for the post office

to deliver it. Let your student count out the correct number of coins to purchase a stamp. Older students may try to see how many different combinations of coins can be used to purchase a stamp, or calculate how much a roll of 100 stamps might cost, or a sheet of 20, etc. Math is important when you want to mail a letter or parcel!

Science: Ants

If possible, obtain an ant farm and let your student send off for the ants! He may even wonder if he will get *aunts* instead! But when the real ants come, he will surely be excited.

There are about 10,000 different kinds of ants that live nearly everywhere on land except areas of extreme cold. Ants, like bees, are fascinating in their life cycles and work habits. With 10,000 different kinds, there is a wide variety of lifestyles and work habits. However, all ants are industrious and work most of the time. Some ants have tunnels underground that have storage areas for seeds and other food, nurseries for young (as they go through the phases of egg, larva, pupa and adult) as well as other rooms.

Take an outing and spend at least 15 minutes or so watching the activity around an anthill. Watch the ants carry bits of material many times their size and see how they accomplish their tasks. The natural activity of "insect" ants mirrors the variety of exuberant activity exhibited by the "aunts" in *Truman's Aunt Farm*.

There are so many fascinating aspects of ant life. If your older student is interested, he might research types of ants with different ways of life. These include: army ants, slave-maker ants, harvester ants, dairying ants, honey ants or fungus growers. Libraries have many books and reference materials to help students at all levels learn about the amazing world of ants! There are also related topics such as ant anatomy, the antlion insect, the animal called an anteater, etc.

Science: Moon and Stars

The last picture of the story shows Aunt Fran and Truman enjoying a quiet moment looking at the moon and stars. Does your student remember what phase this moon is in? If he doesn't, just keep mentioning the information now and then. Without even realizing it your student will continue to pick up more understanding. (The moon at the last picture is a waxing crescent, which means it is "growing" toward a full moon. Information on phases of the moon is found in FIAR Vol. 2, *Owl Moon*.)

Anytime is a wonderful time to enjoy star watching. The glory and the beauty of the skies is breathtaking. Enjoying this beauty together builds an intimacy with your student. Find a dark area, a safe place to sit, use mosquito repellent if necessary, and enjoy the constellations: Cassiopeia, Corona, Cygnus or Draco. Orion is a favorite giant winter constellation. They are all seen in the northern hemisphere. The Southern Cross is a famous constellation seen in the southern hemisphere. See the activity sheets at the end of this unit, called Constellation Viewer and Patterns for Making a Constellation Viewer, for project ideas.

You can also locate the Big and Little Dipper and the North Star, but keep in mind that it may be better just to appreciate the sky for now. Occasionally, you may want to locate and mention a single constellation rather than overwhelm your student with too much information too soon. Your younger student may be less interested in learning the names and locations of constellations than in just enjoying the beauty and time with you. If you are not familiar with the stellar night sky, then learn some of the constellations slowly together and keep the excitement, the wonder, and the fun. There are many library books available on this topic; a good one is *Find the Constellations* by H. A. Rey.

Some cities have planetariums and a field trip to one might be an interesting experience for your older student.

Teacher's Notes

The *Five in a Row* lesson options for each unit in the manual are all you need to teach your child. The additional resource area provided below is simply a place to jot down relevant info you've found that you might want to reference.

TRUMAN'S AUNT FARM

Date: _____

Student: _____

Five in a Row Lesson Topics Chosen:

Social Studies:
_____
_____
_____

Language Arts:
_____
_____
_____

Art:
_____
_____
_____

Math:
_____
_____
_____

Science:
_____
_____
_____

Relevant Library Resources: Books, DVDs, Audio Books

_____
_____
_____
_____
_____
_____
_____

Websites or Video Links:

_____
_____
_____
_____
_____
_____
_____

Related Field Trip Opportunities:
_____
_____
_____

Favorite Quote or Memory During Study:
_____
_____
_____

Constellation Viewer

Take a small, round cardboard oatmeal or cornmeal box and cut a dime-sized eye hole in the middle of the bottom. You will need several tops for your viewer, so keep them as you use the oatmeal and cornmeal and ask friends to save them for you. Each round box top makes a new constellation to view. You may want to learn a new one each time you finish a box of oatmeal! That way you can spread out the information over a longer period of time. If your student loves the constellation "tops" you may find him asking for more oatmeal and oatmeal cookies than usual!

To make the tops, take one star chart from the following page and put it over the lid with the print side touching against the lid. With a sharp nail or ice pick press through the paper and box top making one small hole for each star in the group. Carefully label the lid with the name of the star group and the best viewing months. You can also connect the small lines that show the "picture" of the constellation on the top of the box lid. Then put the lid on the top of the box.

To use the view finder, have your student put his eye to the eye hole (which blocks out most light) and turn toward a light source (lamp, window, etc.) He will be able to see the constellation inside the box. He will see it without all the confusion of the surrounding stars. Later he can look for this simple shape in the night sky and perhaps find it more easily. The lines that help us "see" a picture in the constellations are visible on the outside of the lid (for his reference) but not through the viewer because these lines are not in the sky!!

Each time you obtain a new box top, make an additional constellation top. Get to know the shape and then try looking for it in the evening. There are easy-to-recognize winter constellations too. Orion is the author's favorite! Keep the lids in a shoe box. Let your student cover the box in black paper and decorate with stars.

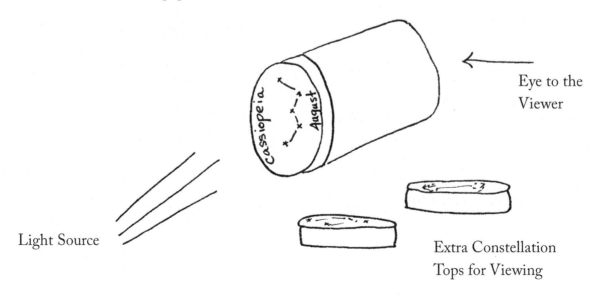

Eye to the Viewer

Light Source

Extra Constellation Tops for Viewing

Patterns for Making Your Constellation Viewer

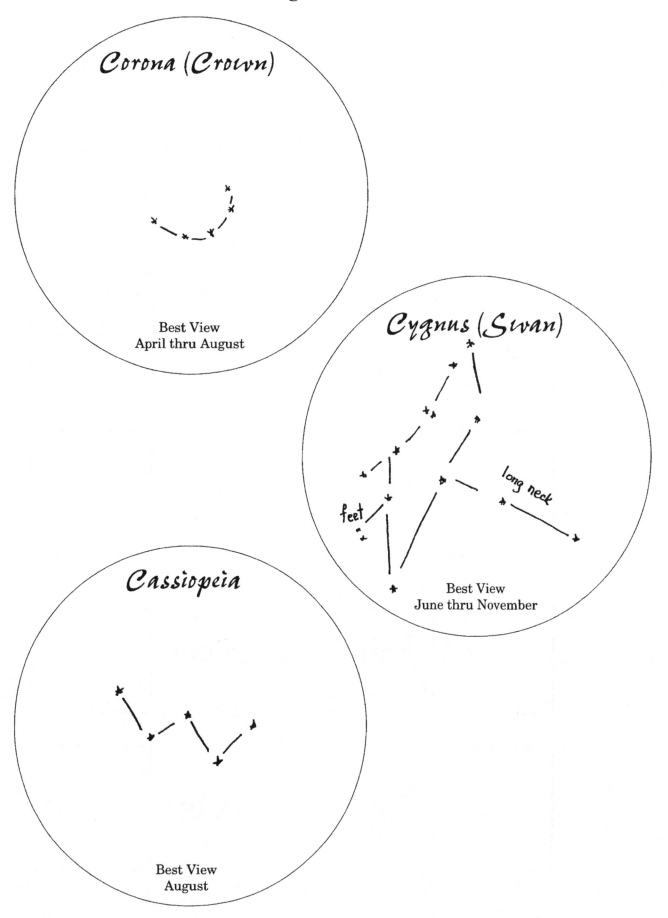

Corona (Crown)

Best View
April thru August

Cygnus (Swan)

long neck

feet

Best View
June thru November

Cassiopeia

Best View
August

Name:

Date:

Language Arts: **Homophones**

Homophones are words that sound alike but are spelled differently and have different meanings.

Draw an image in each box representing the word next to it.

Example

Stair

Stare

104

Hare

Hair

Pair

Pear

Ant

Aunt

The Duchess Bakes a Cake

Title:	*The Duchess Bakes a Cake*
Author:	Virginia Kahl
Illustrator:	Virginia Kahl
Copyright:	1955
Summary:	The cake got baked, but the price was high!

Social Studies: History - Feudal Society

The Duchess Bakes a Cake takes place in the time of kings and queens, dukes and duchesses, knights and castles. This period of time is known as the Middle Ages (or Medieval times). It spans the years from approximately A.D. 400 to the 1500s. Explain to your student the basics of the lifestyle of the time: kings who rule their royal lands; land-wealthy lords who give titles like Duke and Duchess along with grants of land. Explain that the lords and dukes often fight to conquer or keep their land. You may also talk about the slaves and serfs who work the land, and the many brave knights who protect it. Included in this way of life are those in the church: priests, nuns and monks, and the people who give service: bakers, servants, builders, soldiers, etc. Place your story disk on any European country that would be likely to have castles.

Expand any topic as far as you wish for a great time of play and learning. Try using Playmobil® toys or LEGO® bricks to make castles. Or make castles along with other play items from recyclables, such as boxes and cartons, etc. Draw maps of entire estates and all the details they might have. To do this collect several simplified books on the Middle Ages at the library. Let your student look at the pictures for ideas. Using a mural-sized piece of paper for this project, you could work on it for several months. Or make up characters and story scenarios that could have happened in and about your castle. Bind the stories together in a book. Your older student might want to make watercolor or marker illustrations (even pencil sketches) for the story.

Social Studies: Problem Solving

Read the story for the first time, stopping when Gunhilda cries. Ask your student what solutions *she* might think of to solve her problem and get the Duchess down. Then, finish the story and talk about the simplicity of the book's solution. Did your student have any better ideas?

Social Studies: Consequences

Even your young student is not too young to know that certain behaviors bring consequences. In FIAR Vol. 1, Papa Piccolo took responsibility for the kittens and consequently enjoyed love and pride of a family. In FIAR Vol. 2, Peter Rabbit did not listen to his mother and his consequences were fear and illness. In *The Duchess Bakes a Cake*, there are two major consequences. The first is that the Duchess, not being familiar with the ways of baking, greatly overestimates the ingredients in the recipe, especially the leaven. The result is an unusually high cake! Discuss how carefully many cooks measure ingredients and follow recipes. (See more on this subject in the Math lesson for this unit.) Another consequence is that the group that eats the cake becomes quite overweight! Too many calories in a short time has an effect or consequence. Use this opportunity to talk about "consequences," both positive and negative, and be looking for them in other stories.

Language Arts: Poetry and Rhyme Scheme

Virginia Kahl has written a story in rhyming verse. The poem generally follows an AA, BB, CC, etc. rhyming scheme where the first two lines rhyme, then the next two, and so on. When you have read the story poem several times, mention that one reason the poem is pleasant to the ear is the rhyming words. With your student, check the page to see which words are the rhyming words. Together you will discover that the words at the ends of the lines rhyme. (Your student may remember rhyming poems from previous FIAR units such as *Stopping By Woods on a Snowy Evening* from Vol. 1 and *Paul Revere's Ride* earlier in this volume.)

Language Arts: Poetic Device - Alliteration

Alliteration, (uh-lit-ter-AY-shun) is the repetitive beginning consonant sound in lines of poetry. The following refrain (a repetitive line or phrase), that runs throughout the poem is also alliterative:

"You'll all be delighted, for I'm going to make a lovely light luscious delectable cake."

Just mention to your student that the refrain has an interesting sound to it because of the same beginning sounds several times in a row (and also some same internal consonant sounds, called consonance). As a teacher you decide whether to point out the internal "L" sounds in this line or just let the "*lovely light luscious*" words be the lesson for now. There will be time to build slowly and carefully on beginning foundations.

Language Arts: Synonyms

(**Teacher's Note:** This is probably a lesson for your older student.)

As the Duchess' cake started to rise higher and higher, she "pushed it and pummeled it, punched it and pat on it ..." Although each of these words has a slightly different meaning, the words have a similar quality of meaning and could be considered synonymous. **Synonyms** are words having general similar meaning but shades of variation, such as "angry and upset," or "fearful and timid."

Introduce your older student to a children's thesaurus. Let her play with the word meanings and shades of meanings, and find some interesting words to share. Remind her that she can use a thesaurus to find just the right word she's looking for in her writing projects.

"Pushed", "pummeled", "punched" and "pat" are also alliterative words (see previous lesson).

Language Arts: Plot

The action line or plot of a story includes:

Conflict: The problem of the story.

Rising Action: The growing sense of excitement surrounding the problem.

Climax: The high point of excitement.

Denouement: (day-new-MAHN) The resolution of the problem or final outcome. It is sometimes called the falling action.

The Duchess Bakes a Cake has a strong plot line and it might be fun to figure out with your student (let her try to decide, then help if necessary) the plot elements and where they fit the story. Ask your student questions like: "What do you think created the problem in this story?" or "When do you think the excitement began to grow?" "What do you think was the most exciting moment in the story?" "What was the final outcome?" It is fine if your answers are slightly different than the ones below:

Conflict (Problem): The duchess, out of her boredom, decides to bake a light cake. In her zeal she puts in way too much leavening (a rising agent like yeast). The cake, although punched and pummeled, continues to rise with the duchess riding high atop, past the towers of the castle and into the sky.

Rising Action: The duchess' family and the king and queen, desperate to have her down, resort to one rescue attempt after another from a royal command to catapults and arrows, each more dangerous than the one before. Will she ever get down?

Climax: The climax occurs when the last idea has failed. Gunhilda, the baby, begins to cry loudly. No one can stop her and then the answer is found! They begin to eat the cake.

Denouement: The resolution or outcome of the story occurs as the cake is eaten and the duchess descends to the ground. They are happy to have the duchess back, though everyone gains a little weight, and they ask her please not to bake again.

Teacher's Note: In FIAR Vol. 1, there are three stories with good examples of plot lessons that you might want to review: *Lentil*, *Mike Mulligan and His Steam Shovel*, and *Cranberry Thanksgiving*.

Perhaps your student could think of a different "problem" the family could face and make it the conflict of a quick short story of her own. She could include the conflict along with rising action, climax and denouement, writing her story as a **sequel** to *The Duchess Bakes a Cake*. The story would not necessarily have to be in verse.

Language Arts: Cast of Characters

For fun, make a list of the characters in this story. Your list could include, besides the King and Queen and the Duchess' family, the cook, the General, foot soldiers, longbowmen, the housekeeper, Countess, etc. Let your student illustrate the list if she wishes.

Language Arts: Story Ending

When you have finished reading the last page of *The Duchess Bakes a Cake* ask your student if, in her opinion, the story ends happily. (Listen to and enjoy the reasoning of your student—there are no right or wrong answers.)

Virginia Kahl's ending has turned the events back to the beginning. This is one way writers finish a story. Notice the similarity in the first four lines of the last page compared with the second stanza of the first page. The main difference is that now the Duchess has an exciting adventure to remember.

Language Arts: Vocabulary

minstrels   Musicians.

embroidery   Decorative stitching with colored threads on cloth held tight in a hoop.

turret   High, narrow, round towers on a castle.

luscious   Delicious.

pummeled   Pounded or punched.

leaven   An ingredient that makes cakes and breads rise.

rushes   Plant leaves or stems that have (in this story) been woven into rugs or mats.

Art: Drama

This simple story is perfect for dramatic performances. Whether you choose a single scene or attempt to produce the entire story, the humor and simple setting are sure to combine with your student's actions to make a hit!

For instance, if you decide to use only one performer, try the scene where the Duchess makes the cake. You and your student could have quite a hilarious time finding items to represent the ingredients in the cake. Get a very large bowl (or tub!) and use grapes (real or plastic) for the bilberries, marbles for the dogberries, etc. Have an item to correspond to each ingredient. If you can, find a cruet (little pitcher that holds vinegar). Can't you just imagine your student performing the actions as someone reads the words, pretending to pour in some vinegar, maybe a little more, then shrugging and throwing in the entire cruet!

The scene with the Duchess rising higher and higher could easily be accomplished if there is a staircase. The Duchess begins on the lowest step and slowly through the story rises. As the Duchess begins eating down while the others eat up, she can slowly begin to come down the stairs. Outdoor play equipment could also be used, such as a ladder or jungle gym, etc.

Costumes would be easy. Use brown grocery bags decorated to look like the characters in the story with holes cut for the heads and arms. Make sure if you have a Gunhilda, she has a "G" on her costume!

Your older student might like to fashion an actual catapult from boxes for scenery. If, by chance, she makes a working model it could shoot pillows!

If you stage a full production, think about doing invitations and having an audience. You could have a narrator while the actors only pantomime their roles. This might invite less stage fright. It is also possible to narrate most of the story while letting the actors say a few lines like "I'm going to bake a ....", "I want something to eat!" and "My dear you really can make a ...", etc.

Art: Foreshadowing - Catching the Clues

Often, an author will give a hint or clue to the events or outcome of the story and just as often these clues are not caught until the story is ended or reread. Sometimes, an observant reader can pick up a clue. In this case the clue is in the illustrations rather than in the text. Opposite the first page of text, the Duke and the Duchess are shown with their thirteen daughters. Ask your student to look at the picture and see if she can tell the daughters apart. She will probably say the only difference seems to be that the youngest is a bit smaller and she is also the only one with the initial of her name on the front of her dress. Why? This should warn the reader to keep her eye on her, because she may play an important part in this story. This type of lesson is an exercise in observation and the skills gained by learning to observe the world around her may benefit your student throughout her life.

Art: Three-Color Printing and Complementary Colors

The Duchess Bakes a Cake is a work that is printed in three colors of ink: black, red and green. Your student, if she has used FIAR Vol. 1 & 2, has seen monochromatic, one-color printing (*Make Way for Ducklings*), two-color printing (*Down Down the Mountain*), as well as full, four-color illustrations in many stories. Ask her if she thinks it interesting that good illustrations can be in any of these styles. Imaginative figures, action and good drawing are more important in most pictures than the color. Sometimes too much color is even distracting.

The following exercise is to broaden your student's awareness of the importance of good drawing as opposed to using an over abundance of colors. It may also increase her appreciation of all styles of good art. The point can be made with your older student by taking her to a gallery that displays a black and white photography exhibit, or searching online for black and white photos. (Obviously, the subject matter of the exhibit will have to be screened.) What will capture her attention as she gazes at the black and white photographs is facial expression, line, shape, interesting objects, or exciting events. She will find that color is not always a necessity for the enjoyment of art! You may also be able to find black and white photography in books at the library. (Again, the books need to be pre-screened.)

You may also want to mention that when Virginia Kahl chose red and green, she was using complementary colors. Red and green are opposite each other on the color wheel. Complementary colors have a great amount of contrast and make a striking statement when placed close together. Doesn't this seem a good choice for an active story? (See the lesson on complementary colors in FIAR Vol. 1.)

Art: Type Style - Old English

When you look at the picture of the children belonging to the Duke and Duchess, you notice that one outfit is not the same. Gunhilde has a giant "G" printed in an odd script on the front of her dress.

Sometimes children of eight or nine begin to notice and long to imitate unusual scripts or styles of type. If your older student is interested, let him try to imitate this Old English (also called Gothic or Blackletter) style of printing. She may be helped by using paper on which you have drawn light lines about two inches apart. A good roller ball black pen or even a pencil will work for beginning. For an Old English alphabet your student can copy or explore, see the Old English Alphabet activity sheet.

Art: Activities with a Medieval Theme

Using internet resources and library books, explore the making of shields, coats of arms and pennants, visit a museum to see real suits of armor, draw or make castles with turrets (from cardboard or recyclables), draw or make bridges and moats, etc. Read some King Arthur, Robin Hood or other books of the time. You could serve food that was common during the Middle Ages (try a roast turkey drumstick or an English meat pie) or listen to music from that time. You may want to save this story for the end of the school year. That way, these activities can spill into summer play and you'll have even more time to explore many interesting topics from this period. Emphasize hands-on experiences, rather than textbook memorization.

Art: Action

In *The Dutchess Bakes a Cake*, the actions of the Duchess and other figures have variety and simple animation. At the end of this unit, you'll find an activity sheet with stick figure drawings. Using tracing paper, trace the figures on these two pages (or let your older student do this herself). Now let your student try to match your tracings to the figures in the story by laying the marked tracing paper over the book pages until the marks line up and the correct figure is found. (The picture in which the movements of the clothed figure matches the armature stick figure's action.)

This matching game is fun and it provides your student with an exercise in careful observation, actual matching line for line, and abstract matching (seeing the lines of movement through the draping). This activity also provides your student with a beginning lesson in how an artist achieves the action movements in her figures.

Math: The Number Thirteen

Thirteen is an interesting number to discuss. To some people it is a superstitious bad omen (with references appearing many times in literature and media) while to others it is the joy of getting an extra doughnut or bagel at no charge, as in a "baker's dozen."

There are thirteen daughters in *The Duchess Bakes a Cake*. You could ask your older math student to double the number, triple it, quadruple it, etc. This will not only give practice in multiplying but also with terminology like doubling, tripling, etc.

Math: Measuring - Liquid and Dry Ingredients

Ask your student the origin of the problem created by the Duchess as she baked her lovely cake: What happened to the cake and why? (The cake rose higher and higher because the Duchess, completely unfamiliar with cooking, did not measure the ingredients, especially the leaven.*) Talk about cooking and the necessity of following a recipe carefully. While experimenting with new tastes and foods is fun, to get dependable, repeatable results time after time, careful measuring is important until you are completely familiar with the process.

If there is interest, show your student the correct steps to measure dry ingredients with measuring spoons and measuring cups (show her how to level the flour with a knife), and also how to measure liquid ingredients with spoons and liquid cup measures. Let your young student see how many tablespoons of water will make a 1/4 cup, etc. To end your lesson, have fun together and make a lovely light luscious delectable cake the right way! (An angel food cake is quite light.)

[*Lessons on leaven and yeast have been included in *Cranberry Thanksgiving* (FIAR Vol. 1) and *Mrs. Katz and Tush* (FIAR Vol. 2). If you have not covered this material before and wish to introduce this subject to your student, here is brief information: baking powder, baking soda or yeast are all used for leavening (rising action) in different recipes. Baking soda and baking powder work on the basis of chemical reactions. They are alkaline in nature. When some acidic ingredient such as buttermilk, lemon juice, vinegar, etc. is added to the recipe the chemical reaction that results releases tiny gas bubbles that cause the rising action. Yeast, however, is a tiny one-celled plant that actually grows, releasing oxygen bubbles which cause the baked goods to rise.]

Science: Nutrition - Calories

When everyone eats the delicious cake, they consume so much to rescue the Duchess that they all become overweight. You may want to explore the calorie content of various foods with the aid of a simple calorie-counting book from the library or a chart you find online. This is also an excellent time to help your child discover the healthy difference between an apple for a snack and a candy bar. Even if both have a similar number of calories, the natural vitamins and fiber of an apple make it a much better choice than the saturated fats and sugars of a candy bar. Be sure to look up the number of calories in various kinds of cake, as well. Then, just for fun, let your older student estimate how many calories might be in the Duchess' cake!

Teacher's Notes

The *Five in a Row* lesson options for each unit in the manual are all you need to teach your child. The additional resource area provided below is simply a place to jot down relevant info you've found that you might want to reference.

THE DUCHESS BAKES A CAKE

Date: _____

Student: _____

Five in a Row Lesson Topics Chosen:

Social Studies:
_____
_____
_____

Language Arts:
_____
_____
_____

Art:
_____
_____
_____

Math:
_____
_____
_____

Science:
_____
_____

**Relevant Library Resources:
Books, DVDs, Audio Books**
_____
_____
_____
_____
_____
_____

Websites or Video Links:
_____
_____
_____
_____
_____
_____

Related Field Trip Opportunities:
_____
_____
_____

Favorite Quote or Memory During Study:
_____
_____
_____

Old English Alphabet Pattern

A B C D E F G

H I J K L M N

O P Q R S T

U V W X Y Z

Name:

Date:

Math: **Measuring - Liquid and Dry Ingredients**

First you need the correct tools. Liquid measuring cups are used for both liquid and some dry ingredients. They have measurement lines on the side of the cup. When measuring a liquid be sure your eyes are level with the measurement line. For dry ingredients such as flour, use a measuring cup that is metal or plastic, and flat across the top. This is so you can fill the cup and then draw a knife across the top to level off the dry ingredient. Some dry ingredients are not packed (pressed down) into the cup (such as flour), while some are usually packed (such as brown sugar).

Measuring spoons can be used for wet and dry ingredients. You can level off dry ingredients in measuring spoons, too.

Let your student practice measuring liquid and dry ingredients. For a younger student, let them see how many tablespoons are in 1/4 cup.

For your older student, they can see how fractions are involved in baking. Notice how 1/4, 1/3, 1/2, and 1 cup measuring cups relate to one another. Halving a recipe can be excellent practice working with fractions. Find a simple recipe and teach them how to halve an ingredient. Then let them finish halving the recipe. You can also practice adding or multiplying by doubling a recipe.

Name:

Date:

Art: **Action and Body Language**

These skeletal stick figures were made by laying tracing paper over the illustrated figures in the story *The Duchess Bakes a Cake*. On tracing paper, re-trace these skeletal figures using this page as a pattern. Now, lay your tracing paper figures over the illustrations in the story and try to "match" them up with the story's characters.

116

The Duchess Bakes a Cake

Andy and the Lion

Title:	*Andy and the Lion*
Author:	James Daugherty
Illustrator:	James Daugherty
Copyright:	1938
Award:	Caldecott Honor Book
Category:	Classic
Summary:	There is no doubt this story is fiction. It is packed with all the warmth of a country boy—full of life, and of course, a lion!

Social Studies: Geography - Setting

The story is set in Andersonville. (Look at the story's illustration on the first page.) Notice Andy's bare feet and overalls. Notice how Andy is washing up in a bowl. Examine the picket fences and variety of "critters" which all speak of small-town country life some years ago. This small town probably exists before television, Nintendo and movies. Having a circus come to town is extremely exciting and most of the townspeople enjoy watching the entertainment. The state where Andersonville exists is never mentioned, so the story disk can be placed in any state you wish, or in the special space for fictitious settings.

Be sure to notice the two lions on the copyright page and the inscription to them. This is another sight that your student could actually see someday at the entrance to the New York Public Library. Show your student pictures of these famous library lions online, and also see the related Art: Sculpture lesson later in this unit.

Social Studies and Art: History of the Circus and Circus Posters

Remember the circus and performance posters of *Another Celebrated Dancing*

Bear (FIAR Vol. 1), *Mirette on the High Wire* and *Babar, To Duet or Not to Duet* (FIAR Vol. 2), and *Andy and the Circus* (FIAR Vol. 3)? These posters may use color, action or exhilarating words to excite the reader and create a desire in him to buy tickets.

In *Andy and the Lion*, the illustration for Part 3 shows a man using glue and a big brush to put up a poster on a wall. (Some billboard signs are still applied in the same way.) The poster says, "*Greatest ... coming soon*," and has some sort of date on it. Your older student may like to research old circus posters. The history of the circus in the United States is an interesting topic. Historically, many circus acts were brought to the U.S. from European and Asian countries. This makes the study of the circus quite an adventure in geography and culture, too. Your student can also learn how a circus is run and which circuses have been the most famous throughout history. Other aspects of the circus to investigate are the circus train and the opening day circus parade.

Social Studies: Relationship - Inspiration

Ask your student if he remembers who told Andy the tall tales about lions. (Tall tales are stories that become so exaggerated that they are no longer true. It was Andy's grandfather that told him the stories.) What was the result of these wild stories? (Andy dreamed about hunting lions in Africa.) Does your student know any family members that can tell a great story? Is there anyone whom he finds inspirational when it comes to stories that excite or entertain? Does your student tell imaginative stories himself?

Language Arts: Aesop's Fable - Kindness

After you have read the story to your student several times, find and read the fable of Aesop called The

Lion and the Mouse. In this story the lion spares the mouse's life and the mouse returns the kindness. Discuss the ways this story and the story *Andy and the Lion* are similar and different. Each story demonstrates that kindness is a good investment.

Ask your student if he has ever had a similar situation (probably not with lions!) and share any memories you might have of a kindness repaid.

Language Arts: Openings and Closings

A story's opening sentence needs to be well-written to immediately catch the reader's interest. Gather a pile of books: picture books and classics like *Treasure Island*, *Swiss Family Robinson*, *Little Women*, etc. Read just the first one or two sentences. Ask your student if he thinks the sentence sounds interesting. He will probably like some and not be too excited about others. However, he will enjoy the fact that you ask his opinion and let him decide what he likes.

Then, read the first sentence of *Andy and the Lion* again. Ask your student if it draws him in (does he want to know what happens next?) because it is well-written and interesting. Remind him that good openers are an important part of writing and add "Good Opening" to the list of Choices a Writer Can Make.

A good writer also wraps up the tale. He writes an ending that ties back into the beginning and finishes or closes the story. Ask your student if he thinks James Daugherty did this. (In the beginning, *Andy and the Lion* shows Andy on his way to the library, while the last illustration shows Andy returning his lion book to the library as the little sign now reads: The End.) Remind your student that stories (and later, essay-type articles and news articles) need good opening sentences and a closing that tie back in to the beginning and complete the work. Add "Good Closure" to list of Choices a Writer Can Make.

Language Arts: Layout of Text

The sentences of this story aren't complete on each page. In order to finish the sentence, the reader has to turn the page and continue to read. What is going to happen next remains a mystery until you turn the page. This type of text layout is effective in pulling the reader into the story. Your older student may want to write a story with pages that turn like a book, and have the text laid out in this manner.

Language Arts: Vocabulary

cautiously   Very slowly and carefully.

investigate   Look carefully for clues and make observations.

famous   Well known.

Language Arts and Art: Personification

Both the words of the text and the illustration personify the sun on the thirteenth page of the story. The text reads: "The sun was looking in at the window...," and the picture of the sun has a face and personality. Personification is fun to use in both writing and illustrating. Your student could try some of each. Make sure "Personification" is on the list of Choices a Writer Can Make and Choices an Artist Can Make.

Art: Foreshadowing in Illustration

Foreshadowing gives the reader a clue to future events of the story and can come from either the text or the illustration. In *Andy and the Lion*, an observant reader might catch the newspaper headline on p. 7. If he notices this piece of foreshadowing, he will know that the tail Andy sees sticking out from behind a rock is probably the escaped lion. If the reader misses the clue, then he is surprised when the lion appears. Foreshadowing is an advanced topic. The reason for mentioning it here is the emphasis on the fun of observation, not imitation. However, if your student hears this technique mentioned from

Art: Action in Figures

From the front cover of the book to the back cover, every illustration is full of action—dramatic, moving action. Andy's exceptional, bursting-out love of life, the incredible enjoyment of everything around him, and his love of adventure come spilling out in every illustration. Look with your student for pictures with exceptional dramatic movement. (Andy waving good-bye to his mother before school—he could get an Oscar for that performance! Remember too, the heart-wrenching series of illustrations when Andy is removing the thorn from the lion's paw!) How much force does it look like it takes to remove the thorn? How does the artist show it takes a lot? (Notice the lines that look like a sprung spring. How many times do Andy and the lion tumble end over end?) Whether animal or human, Daugherty's illustrated action is superb.

Look with your student specifically at the arms, fingers, toes and the facial expressions of the story characters. Ask your older student if he would like to try drawing a hand or foot with "movement."

Art: Two-Color Printing

Ask your student what colors Daugherty used to illustrate *Andy and the Lion*. (Yellowish tan and black.) Virginia Kahl, in *The Duchess Bakes A Cake*, uses three-color printing: red, green and black. Daugherty has chosen a two-color printing. The red, green and black ink worked well for Kahl's book. So, too, the black and predominantly yellow-tan are both dramatic and full of warmth for this story. The black is dramatic portraying Andy's vi-

tality and the lion's strength, while the yellow-tan symbolizes the warmth of feeling between Andy and his world and his lion.

Let your student try a two-color illustration to a favorite story.

Art: Hide and Seek - Hidden Animals

Have your young student try finding all the "critters" in the double page illustration of Part 2. (There are at least twelve.)

For your older student: When Andy first spots the lion, all he sees is the tail and he can't tell what it is. The rest of the animal is hidden from Andy's sight behind a rock. Let your student try drawing something that is mostly hidden. It could be any kind of animal behind a door, tree, rock, etc. You might possibly see only part of the face, the tail or even just the middle portion of the animal!

Art: Surface Lines

Surface lines are a function of perspective in that they cause a flat surface to appear rounded and three dimensional. The illustrator, James Daugherty, uses a multitude of surface lines and you can point out this effect on nearly any page. If your student has interest, let him begin to see the results of using surface lines to make a circle look like a ball or make a rolling pin look round by drawing the curving lines on simple line objects.

Art: Line of Design

Notice the children on the Part 3 page in a giant "S" line of design following the circus news as if the were following the Pied Piper. The "S" shape is backwards but it is the "S" line of design. There are other "S" lines of design in the illustrations. Ask your student to hunt for them. (Illustration with the text: "The grateful lion licked Andy's face to show how pleased he was." Look at the tip of the lion's tail, around the lion's body, through Andy and around the book-string to the books. Also, trace the S-curve on the next page: "But it was time to part." In addition, notice the illustration with the text: "Andy stood in front of the Lion and shouted to the angry people." Each of these illustrations follow the "S" shaped line.)

Draw a long "S" shape *lightly* on paper. Let your student draw or print pictures that he can glue on the line of design. Learning to have a framework (design line) for compositions is an advanced skill but it can be introduced in this way just for fun. (The pencil line can be carefully erased when the work is complete, if necessary.) File the pictures in his notebook for his own review later.

Art: Cover - Diagonal Line of Design

Look at the cover of *Andy and the Lion*. You see three figures, in a diagonal line with the largest at the top and the smallest at the bottom. This is reminiscent of the cover of *Storm in the Night*, FIAR Vol. 1. If you happen to own *Storm in the Night*, discuss the similarities and differences of the cover illustration with your student. Let him try to fashion a similar line of design using three items on a diagonal line. Have him use printed figures or draw the items. Remember that overlapping is fine and works especially well when gluing three items together. Keep these pictures in his notebook.

Art: Sculpture - Appreciation

Turn to the copyright page of the story and study the picture of the statues of the library lions. Look online for actual pictures of the New York Public Library and you'll see first that there really are statues of lions at that location! Second, you can tell James Daugherty drew his Lady Astor and Lord Lenox with a lot of "added" personality.

Encourage your student to look for statues and sculptures in his neighborhood and city or town. Are there any lion statues? If not, what kinds of figures are there? Through good books, your student will be exposed to many different forms of painting, drawing, collages, etc., but sculpture is another fascinating form of art that can be loved and appreciated from a very young age if it is brought to your student's attention.

Math: Counting

There are many varieties of items your student can count such as animals (critters) or pickets on a fence, etc. Counting the pictures of "books" in all the illustrations is fun as well as counting different occupations. Some occupations might include lawn keeper, librarian, policeman, butcher, mayor, band leader and the variety of circus performers and workers.

Science: Lions and Natural History

The illustrations show Andy getting the book about lions from the Natural History section of the library. Natural History is the general subject of nature and its history. There are museums of natural history and books on natural history. There are naturalists, who study natural history. If your student loves the world of nature around him, then he, too, is a naturalist. Help your student locate the Natural History section in your local library the next time you go there and look at the wide variety of subjects included in this general section. Maybe there is a Museum of Natural History near your home. If so, plan a field trip!

Science: Dreams

After reading about Andy's dream of lion hunting bring up a discussion about dreams. Talk with your student about the fact that most people have dreams and that some are funny and some scary, etc. Remember the young Babar's dream in FIAR Vol. 2, *Babar, To Duet or Not to Duet*? It seems to be caused by a guilty conscience. But Andy's dream looks as if it is encouraged by his reading and the exciting tall tales his grandpa tells him.

You could bring up the idea that we also use the word "dream" to speak of hopes, as in "hopes and dreams to do something." One might say, "I have a dream to build my own tree house," or "My dream is to learn to ride a bicycle," etc.

Teacher's Notes

The *Five in a Row* lesson options for each unit in the manual are all you need to teach your child. The additional resource area provided below is simply a place to jot down relevant info you've found that you might want to reference.

ANDY AND THE LION

Date: _____

Student: _____

Five in a Row Lesson Topics Chosen:

Social Studies:
_____
_____
_____

Language Arts:
_____
_____
_____

Art:
_____
_____
_____

Math:
_____
_____
_____

Science:
_____
_____
_____

**Relevant Library Resources:
Books, DVDs, Audio Books**

_____
_____
_____
_____
_____
_____
_____

Websites or Video Links:

_____
_____
_____
_____
_____
_____
_____

Related Field Trip Opportunities:
_____
_____
_____

Favorite Quote or Memory During Study:
_____
_____
_____

124

Name:

Date:

Art: **Sculpture - Appreciation**

Sculpture Scavenger Hunt

Encourage your student to look for statues and sculptures in his neighborhood and city or town. Are there any lion statues? If not, what kinds of figures are there? This can be a day trip search or an ongoing hunt. If you can get close enough to the statues, snap a picture to paste into the frames below. Also keep a tally at the bottom of the page to track your ongoing total.

Tally

The illustrations show Andy getting the book about lions from the Natural History section of the library. Natural History is the general subject of nature and its history. There are museums of natural history and books on natural history. There are naturalists, who study natural history.

Virtual 🖥 FIELD TRIP

Search online for a virtual tour of the Smithsonian Museum of Natural History. You will find an index of available virtual tours through rooms and select exhibits within the Natural History building as well as through satellite support stations.

Choose one or two exhibits to explore and dictate, write or draw notes or sketches below to document your virtual field trip.

126

Go-Along Movie: Night at the Museum is based on the American Museum of Natural History in New York City.

Andy and the Lion

Name:

Date:

Social Studies: **Storytelling Inspiration**

Interesting pictures are a great way to inspire an exciting or unique story. Have your student make up a story based on the three images below (one story including all three images). They can write it themselves or you can write it out for them to keep in a notebook.

Daniel's Duck

Title:	*Daniel's Duck*
Author:	Clyde Robert Bulla
Illustrator:	Joan Sandin
Copyright:	1979
Summary:	A true artist wants to create. He thinks his project over carefully, and often has deep feelings about it!

Social Studies: Geography - State of Tennessee

Use just the bits and pieces of the following information that your student will enjoy: The setting for *Daniel's Duck* is a log cabin on a mountain in the state of Tennessee. Tennessee is in the eastern half of the United States. It has eight states that border it (tied with Missouri for most bordering states) and the Appalachian Mountain chain running through the eastern half of the state. So the setting for *Daniel's Duck* is probably in eastern Tennessee. The rest of the land slopes gradually downward as it moves toward the Mississippi River on Tennessee's western border. Tennessee is known in American History for being the birthplace of Davy Crockett (1786-1836), the site of the Civil War Battle of Shiloh in 1862 and the home of three U.S. Presidents: Andrew Jackson, James K. Polk and Andrew Johnson.

Place the story disk on Tennessee.

Social Studies: Mountain Cabin and Small Town Culture

Leaf with your student through pp. 5-29 and make a list of all the aspects of country "cabin life" that you see: log cabin with white chinking, rocking chairs on the porch, split rail fences, mules to ride, washing kettle outside, pigs, chickens, cats and dogs, bare feet and overalls, spinning wheel, woven bottom chairs, dulcimer, cast iron pans to use on the wood-burning cookstove, crocks, oil lamp, fiddle, quilting frame that lets down from the ceiling, large washtubs to bathe in, a wagon to get to town, etc.

In order to teach early classifying skills, you could also split your list something like the following, giving your student four different areas in which to hunt for and place items. For your non-reader, just have her look and tell you what to write down, then read the different lists to her so she can decide where each item fits. Then, encourage her for the number of different items she finds.

Home & Outdoors	Furniture & Furnishings
Log Cabin	Rocker
Stone Fireplace	Woven chair
Porch	Bellows
Split-rail fence	Plank table
Iron wash kettle	Oil lamp
Wagon	Quilting frame
	Cook stove
	Broom
	Spinning wheel
	Crocks
	Cradle
	Wash tub
	(many more items on walls and floor)

Music & Art	Livestock & Pets
Fiddle	Pigs
Dulcimer	Chickens
Carving	Mules
Moccasins	Horses
Quilt	Cats and dogs
Dolls	

The clothes and methods of transportation seen in the illustrations place the story somewhere around the 1890s. Did your student see any automobiles or machines in the illustrations? This, too, helps fix the date. Look at the house on p. 51 of the story. Are there old farm houses that look something like this where your student lives? Can you find out when they were built?

Social Studies: Climate - Long Winters

In the mountains of Tennessee, Daniel's family spends a long, somewhat isolated winter. It is during this time they make the items to take to the fair in the spring. Discuss with your student how she thinks it would be to live in a cabin for a whole winter and not see anyone but her own family. There is special book called *Snowed In* by Barbara M. Lucas that tells of a long winter in Wyoming in the year 1915. The father gets books and paper so his family can have school at home while they are snowbound. Your student might enjoy hearing this story about a time when homeschooling was a necessity and not a choice!

Social Studies: The County Fair

The county fair was a special event each year. People dressed up, rode into town and gathered to visit and talk to friends and relatives. They came to trade goods and stock up on items which had run out during the winter. They came to see all the wonders that were displayed, and to bring the best of what they had produced, hoping to win a ribbon in the contests. (Remember in FIAR Vol. 2, *Down Down the Mountain*, by Ellis Credle, when the children's fat, juicy turnip wins the contest at the county fair? Remember how hard they worked to grow the turnips?) In this story, Daniel's family works hard to make beautiful things to take to the fair. Ask your student if she can recite what each family member makes. (Father makes moccasins. Mother sews a quilt. Jeff carves a box with little moons on the lid. Daniel fashions a duck looking back.) Also, look at the pictures and text on pp. 38-39, name the things on display at this fair. (Pictures, quilts, rugs, baskets, dolls, coonskin caps, wood carvings, etc.)

Some small towns have fairs. Sometimes there are county fairs and many states have their own state fairs. If you can take your student to a good fair she will see produce—the best that has been grown, prize-winning livestock such as horses, cows, goats, rabbits, pigs, etc., and sections with handmade items, artwork and quilts, baskets, etc., as well as preserved food, like pickles and jams. Often there is an amusement ride section, too.

There is a great deal to observe and learn at a fair, along with a lot of fun! See newborn bunnies, chicks and piglets, and ride the Ferris wheel while eating some cotton candy! If your student is interested, she may want to research acceptable items and make something for the fair. (The 4-H organization could be helpful in her research.)

(For your older student, the story *Charlotte's Web*, by E. B. White, tells of a fair with much humor and poignancy. It might also be an excellent read-aloud book for your family.)

Social Studies: Emotions

When Daniel believes everyone is making fun of his duck, he grabs the duck and runs. Daniel, who has been a confident artist, proud of his work, suddenly feels the duck is no longer good. Was the duck carving no longer good? (It hadn't changed. Daniel's feelings about it had changed.)

Can your student name the emotions that flood over Daniel? (He wants to escape and hide because of his **embarrassment** and **hurt**. (Look at the expression on Daniel's face p. 47.) Then he becomes **angry**. Last, he tries to **destroy** the carving by throwing it into the river. Who helps Daniel deal with his embarrassed, angry and destructive feelings? (Mr. Pettigrew) Does your student think that Daniel's father or friend would have been able to help as much? Why? (Maybe not. Mr. Pettigrew could help because he knew! He was an artist—an expert. He could see that the carving was good, even if it was done by a young artist, and Daniel believed him.)

Ask your student how she would feel if someone laughed at her work, whether artwork, school work, how she cleaned her room, played ball, etc. Talk a bit about the fact that everyone experiences ridicule from time to time. The way one handles it is important. To keep focused on the truth (one's own worth) in the midst of teasing is an important skill of maturity.

If possible, share an embarrassing or hurtful moment of your own with your student. Perhaps something that happened when you were in school. Help her see that while it seemed so important then, one does get over the hurt and learn to take ridicule less seriously.

Language Arts: Comprehension

Ask your student why Daniel did not recognize Henry Pettigrew when he first stopped him at the river and talked with him. (Because p. 9 says that even though Daniel had seen Mr. Pettigrew's work, he had never seen the man himself. Daniel lived on the mountain and Mr. Pettigrew lived in the valley.) Again, it is fun for observant readers to see the clothes and mustache behind the hat on p. 9 and be first to recognize him again on p. 50. For your young student, show her the picture on p. 57 where Daniel finds out who the man is and then flip to p. 9 and let him note the same details—it is Mr. Pettigrew!

Can your student explain what Jeff meant when he said, "It takes more than a good knife and some wood to carve something"? (He meant that one has to either learn how or know how; just having the materials doesn't make an artist. Does your student think this is true? Many people could be handed wood and knives and not know how to carve at all.)

Language Arts: Quotation Marks

After you have read the story through, turn with your student to p. 26 and let her notice the many lines that have quotation marks. Explain that quotation marks are set on each side of a quotation and help the reader know when a character is speaking. Your nonreader can just notice what the marks look like and may bring the subject up when she sees them again, even in other books or magazines, etc. Your young reader will begin to appreciate recognizing these marks and it might even help to have her copy out a short sentence or two from the story to better understand how the marks work and the comma that is necessary inside the closing quote before the speaker's name.

Art: Artists

The charm of *Daniel's Duck* lies in the beginning desire to *be* an artist and the growth of Daniel *as* an artist:

Daniel thinks he's ready to try carving an animal out of wood. He overcomes his brother's discouraging remarks and declares with quiet confidence that he knows how. His father shows wisdom by not entering the argument. Rather, Daniel's father gives him a chance to find out if he can make a wood carving by himself.

The next clue to Daniel's young talent is the way he waits and thinks about what he is going to carve. A block of wood is not like a slate. You can't carve for a time and then decide you don't like it and erase. Daniel knows that for carving he has to have a specific idea to work on before he begins. He patiently waits for that idea to take shape in his mind before he puts the knife to the wood.

Artists often try to show common objects from different angles and points of view. Daniel chooses to carve his duck looking back. That is a more difficult task because it is not the common way to see it. Daniel takes a chance at something different. He can see what it will look like in his imagination. A good artist will often take chances.

Again, Daniel resists becoming discouraged with his brother's comments about how the duck is progressing. The young artist knows what he is doing. His father again backs him up, saying, "Let him do it his way."

The most difficult hurdle, however, proves to be the reaction of the people at the fair. As Daniel sees the people laughing at his work, he loses confidence, grabs the duck and runs. Confidence is restored to the young artist when the veteran artist, Henry Pettigrew, assures him that his work is good. Mr. Pettigrew even asks if he can buy the duck, and Daniel, trusting in the older man's appreciation for the carving, gives the duck away! (Artists often admire other artists' works and enjoy owning them.)

Ask your student if she has had any experiences like Daniel. If she is interested, have her write or dictate a story in which someone makes fun of or seems to make fun of her. Let her show how she did react or how she thinks she would react.

Art: Carving

Have your young student look back at the pictures of toys on pp. 42, 43 and 48. If she could have one of them, which would she choose and why would she like that particular toy?

Carving figures is a difficult task. It has been said the way one carves a deer, for instance, is to cut away everything that isn't a deer! That is much easier said than done. (Look at the carving of the toy on p. 42. The rectangular box with the balls inside is made by carefully carving away the area around the balls and keeping enough of the sides so that the balls won't fall out.)

Carving or sculpting is difficult because it moves beyond the two dimensions of drawing or painting (the paper has height and width) to the three-dimensional realm of height, width and depth. If your student is inspired by the story of *Daniel's Duck* and wants to try some carving, large bars of Ivory® soap are usually soft enough for a beginner to try a project. Large shapes like a fish or whale, a banana, a huddled duck or curled up bunny are easier than intricate objects. Try drawing a "top view," "side view" and both "end views" onto the bar of soap before you begin carving.

If you don't feel comfortable with your student trying the soap carving, decide on a subject together. Show her how you draw the picture of the subject on a cardboard box. Now draw the same pictures on the bar of soap and carve the subject yourself while she watches. You can even ask her, now and then, where she thinks the piece should be cut next. Let your student participate as much as possible, even if she isn't doing the actual carving. She will be amazed as an object "appears" from the bar of soap!

Math: Measuring

When you read about the arts and crafts projects in *Daniel's Duck*, take the opportunity to discuss different measurements. For instance, find a block of wood like Daniel uses for his duck and measure the length, width and depth in inches, etc. The quilting that Daniel's mother does takes yardage of cloth (as well as small scraps) which can be measured in yards, feet and inches, etc.

Science: Winter - Long Nights

(**Teacher's Note:** Solstice and equinox dates vary from year to year. The dates in this lesson are approximate; many calendars will note the exact dates for the current year.)

After reading the story through, turn to p. 15. It says, "It was winter. The nights were long." Ask your student if she is aware of differing lengths of day and night from season to season. You can discuss the fact that days (hours of daylight) become longer and nights shorter from December 21 until June 21 each year. Then from June 21 until December 21 the days (hours of daylight) become shorter and nights longer. For your older student, you can explain that we call those dates (June 21 and Dec. 21) the summer and winter solstice (SOUL-stis) which signifies the longest and shortest days of the year.

You may also want to explain that on March 21 and September 21, the hours of daylight and darkness are exactly equal. We call these days the equinox (EE-qui-nox). March 21 is called the vernal equinox (vernal meaning spring) and September 21 is the autumnal equinox (autumnal meaning fall). If your older student is interested, she can do a great deal of self-directed study and research. Using library books and the internet, she can learn more about the earth's rotation around the sun and how it affects the length of daylight and darkness, the seasons, daylight savings time, etc.

Science: Seasons - Spring

Long lists of sights, sounds, smells and tastes could be made about spring, as well as spring activities. Or, have your student make a collage-type picture about her feelings regarding spring. She could use some paint or markers, and then paste or draw pictures of spring flowers, spring activities, etc. Even torn paper figures of kites, baby bunnies, baseball pictures, or whatever spring means to her, can be used.

In this story, p. 31 shows a spring activity. Ask your student if she knows what it is—spring plowing. For your reading student, have her try an original spring acrostic poem. For instance:

S un feeling warmer
P retty flowers
R ain showers
I nstant growth
N ests with eggs
G reening up everywhere

Teacher's Notes

The *Five in a Row* lesson options for each unit in the manual are all you need to teach your child. The additional resource area provided below is simply a place to jot down relevant info you've found that you might want to reference.

DANIEL'S DUCK

Date: _____

Student: _____

Five in a Row Lesson Topics Chosen:

Social Studies:
_____
_____
_____

Language Arts:
_____
_____
_____

Art:
_____
_____
_____

Math:
_____
_____
_____

Science:
_____
_____
_____

Relevant Library Resources: Books, DVDs, Audio Books

_____
_____
_____
_____
_____
_____
_____

Websites or Video Links:

_____
_____
_____
_____
_____
_____
_____
_____

Related Field Trip Opportunities:
_____
_____
_____

Favorite Quote or Memory During Study:
_____
_____
_____

Name:

Date:

Social Studies: **Emotions**

Below is is a list of emotions. Have your younger student guess the emotions. An older student can guess or act out the emotions.

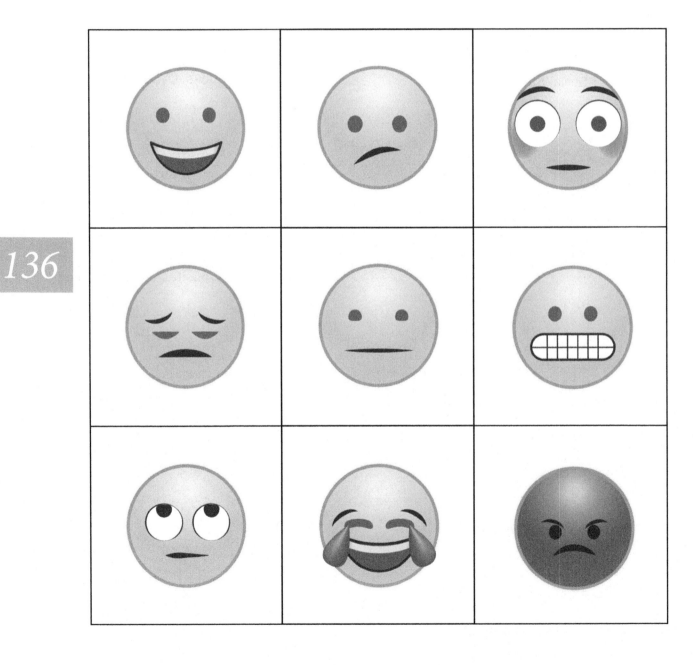

Add these cards to your charades/vocabulary deck for storage and review.

Name:

Date:

Science: **Seasons - Spring**

Create an acrostic poem for the word SPRING.

Decorate your poem with drawings or pictures of what spring means to you!

S _____

P _____

R _____

I _____

N _____

G _____

Name:

Date:

Geography: **Tennessee Flag**

The flag of Tennessee has a field of red, a round emblem in the middle, and a blue stripe running vertically on the fly end. The emblem is a blue circle with three white stars representing the Grand Divisions of the state (West Tennessee, Middle Tennessee, and East Tennessee). *For more information, see Parts of a Flag on page 224.*

Color in the Tennessee flag below.

Warm as Wool

Title:	*Warm as Wool*
Author:	Scott Russell Sanders
Illustrator:	Helen Cogancherry
Copyright:	1992
Summary:	A woman of vision and financial wisdom faces a need, which results in a herd of sheep and warm children.

(**Teacher's Note:** The prologue to this story is like a small story in itself. The description of the journey and of each individual child is worth taking time to savor. You might try reading the prologue to your student on two days preceding the week's lessons. Perhaps you could read it on Saturday and Sunday, stating that it is a preview of the next week's story you are going to do together. This **pre-reading of the prologue** serves as a whetting of your student's interest. It also gives both of you time to enjoy the description of the writing. When you finally begin the story, the characters will already be familiar and the story will not be so long.)

Social Studies: Covered Wagons

The picture above the prologue shows the Ward family in a wooden wagon with canvas stretched over hoops and attached to the sides. This might be considered the 1800s version of the "U-Haul® Rental Truck" in which many people move today. These wagons carried kegs of flour, salted meats, dried beans and as many personal belongings, clothes, blankets, tools and pieces of furniture as could be carried. Your student may be able to imagine the wagons could not carry a great deal (they are smaller than we sometimes think of them) and many special possessions had to be left behind.

The wagons were pulled by horses or oxen and the family would often walk alongside. (Walking was easier on the body than the bumpy ride mile after mile!) These wagons could cover about twelve to fifteen miles in a day.

According to the prologue, the Wards left Connecticut in September. They must have traveled through October and November to reach Ohio and then lived all of December in a lean-to while they built their log cabin. In any case, almost two months on the road, in a rackety wagon, in a tippy boat, and squishing through mud would be a long time. What is the longest trip your student can remember? Did he get tired of the travel? Has he ever moved across country? Share with him any experiences you might have had.

Your older student might like to build a replica covered wagon from cardboard or wood, and research the construction details. He may also want to learn more about what was carried inside. An easy way to construct a simple wagon is to use a round oatmeal box, cut in half lengthwise as the arched wagon canvas. Then insert it into a smaller, rectangular box, or build a "wagon" from cardboard or construction paper. Your student can paint the wagon appropriate colors, etc.

Place the story disk on Ohio, or on Connecticut with a string marker to Ohio.

Social Studies: Relationships - Suffering

According to Scott Russell Sanders in a note after the story's end, "suffering is part of the truth about the American frontier. The settlers suffered, the native people suffered, the woods and soils and wild beasts suffered ... Children [he believes] can understand this if we are honest with them." He goes on to say, "I hope that children will shiver when they hear this story ... I hope they will rub their faces against wool sweaters, hug some patient grown-up about the knees, look for tiny lost things in the grass ... and as they listen, I hope these children will climb into the arms of someone who loves them, and grow warm."

Mr. Sanders captures an important point about suffering: it happens. Each life has some suffering and children can learn to accept the reality of this facet of life, if told in an honest, yet loving, way. They can begin to identify with these story characters and feel the reality of being cold, being disappointed and being discouraged, if they are told by someone they trust and from whom they can receive a reassuring hug. Watching story characters suffer hardships and yet make it through serves as a model for the difficulties in our own lives, and the confidence that we too can make it. And identifying with these characters also cultivates compassion for others who suffer. Ask your student how he might feel if he woke up to frost on his floor. Has he ever experienced a time outdoors or during a power failure that was unusually cold? Do you have any stories to share with him?

Social Studies: Geography and History

With your student, make a map for his notebook that traces the trip Betsy and Josiah Ward's family made in 1803 from Connecticut to Ohio. Be sure to include wagoning through New York State, crossing Lake Erie and landing near Cleveland with as many illustrations as you like. You could work on this project for a short time each day during the week.

[**Teacher's Information: Lake Erie** is one of the Great Lakes that borders the northern part of the United States. The other **Great Lakes** include **Superior, Michigan, Huron**, and **Ontario**. At the time of this story, there was no Erie Canal. Yet just twenty-two years later in 1825 the canal was completed. Planned and promoted by De Witt Clinton, the Erie Canal connects by a series of locks, the city of Albany and Troy on the Hudson River to the city of Buffalo (on Lake Erie). This canal joins the great lakes with the Hudson River and ultimately the Atlantic Ocean. The completion of the Erie Canal promoted the development of New York City as a trade and financial center. Again, this is just additional information for the teacher in case you or your student want to pursue the topic of canals. The Erie Canal was not in existence during the time setting of this story.]

Social Studies: Character - Prudence, Vision and Perseverance

In the character of Betsy Ward (based on a real person), you see a woman that is **prudent**. Talk with your student about what prudent means (carefully managing resources; thrifty, wise). Discuss the fact that Betsy Ward thinks about needing sheep and saves money to buy them. This occurs before they begin their westward journey. She is a prudent woman. When they arrive in Ohio there are no sheep. Rather than spend the money, she continues to save it, never wavering from her intent to "have" sheep.

She also was a woman of **vision**. Betsy can look at a herd of dirty, burr-filled sheep and "see" beyond the problems to the clothes that will come from them. This ability to see the future benefits keeps her from being discouraged about the condition of the sheep. (You might get a discussion going by talking about someone buying an antique car or truck because he "sees it" all shiny and restored in his mind, long before the job is complete. People also buy old houses because they can imagine what they'd look like fixed up. Your student might have found an old piece of junk that someone threw away, for which he could immediately "see" an important use and value. Explain to your student that this is having "vision" for the project, just like Betsy Ward.)

Ask your student what it is that keeps Betsy Ward intent on raising sheep? (Her children are cold.) Even though the death of several sheep brings discouragement, Betsy Ward does not give up. **Perseverance**, the drive to keep going even in the face of discouragement, is a wonderful character quality. Most famous inventions were successfully developed only after many failures by men and women with perseverance. Remember Papa Bleriot in *The Glorious Flight*? (FIAR Vol. 1) Many goals that have worth (like the clothes for the cold children) are achieved through steady perseverance.

[**Teacher's Note:** You may or may not want to comment on the fact that Betsy Ward is quick to judge Mr. Culver for letting his sheep die. He may have been extra careless with his animals, but Betsy finds out that raising sheep in the wild is not an easy task. She has to learn many times from her mistakes. Do you think, perhaps, she feels differently about Mr. Culver by the end of the story?]

Social Studies: Log Cabin Life

(**Teacher's Note:** In FIAR Vol. 2, a lesson for *Down Down the Mountain* discusses that the idea for log cabins came from the Swedish, German, Swiss and Scandinavian immigrants and spread throughout the westward expansion because trees were so plentiful.)

Leaf through the illustrations. Notice, with your student, all the aspects of cabin life that you can find. Observe the shape of the log cabin, the long, sloping roof and the few, small windows. The windows usually had no glass and were often covered in an oiled paper which let in a little light. Other times, they were covered with skins or cloth. Look at the white chinking between the logs and the dirt floor. In the first picture after the log cabin, let your student point out items: stool, bench, butter churn, table, sewing box, etc. Continue with the next page adding: spinning wheel, split-log benches, pitcher, pails, a basket ... and throughout the story with: brooms, axes, barrels, carding combs, wash tubs, a wheelbarrow, a loom, etc.

The picture on the cover of the book shows Betsy Ward and her sheep in front of a split rail fence. This type of fence was often used in the times of the pioneers. Your student may see fences like this on shows or movies about pioneer life. He may also see such fences at parks or in some yards and he will be able to see how they are constructed.

Together, the front and back cover of this story make one complete illustration. Unfold the book so that your student can see the lovely picture. In this picture, one of Ward's sons is carrying two pails of water. (Can your student remember his name? Joshua—it is found in the prologue) What is the device that makes this job easier? (A yoke, which distributes the weight of the pails of water across his shoulders, instead of having to use just his arms. There are other types of yokes, like those used on the oxen, which you might mention.)

Language Arts: Descriptive Language

Scott Russell Sanders has written a book that he hopes will not only teach children about history, but also let them "see, hear, feel, taste and touch," the life of long ago. He writes, "Every child I know loves the sound and weight and taste of words. So I give them *rackety* and *squished*, *ragamuffin* and *pantaloons*."

He's given them a lot more. Sanders' writing is full of words to make the scenes come alive for your student. When you read words like "squished through the mud," let your voice dwell on the words, drawing them out slightly and helping your student "feel" the action. This is a good story to exercise your dramatic reading ability and help the story come alive for your student.

Language Arts: Book Jackets, Prologue and Author's Note

Show your older student that he can usually find additional information about the author and illustrator as well as a synopsis of the story on the book's jacket (or on the inside covers, if paperback). But, in this story, there is also an interesting prologue (which covers a span of time and includes many background details in a short space before the actual story begins), and a lengthy note from the author, explaining in his own words what he hoped to accomplish with this book.

Just helping your student become aware of these different places (prologues, author's notes, book jackets) to find information increases his ability to research his own interest topics. It will encourage him with the knowledge of where to look for answers to his own questions.

Language Arts: Remembering What You've Read

Ask your student if he can remember where Betsy Ward gets the money for her sheep. Where does she get a spinning wheel and loom to make the clothes? (She saves the money before her journey to Ohio, and she brings the loom and spinning wheel from her old home in Connecticut.)

Just learning to pronounce the words by sounding them out isn't the final goal of reading. Comprehension and memory are important parts of reading. Look for opportunities to "review" what you and your student have been reading. This simple process reinforces the fact that comprehension and retention are a vital part of the reading process.

Language Arts: Poetic Prose - Simile

The author has used a type of figurative language called a simile (SIM-uh-lee) in *Warm as Wool*. In the prologue, he describes how the waves were bucking under them "*like* wild horses," and how William was "quick *as* a fox." Discuss with your student how comparing one thing to another brings imagery and life to the story. It lets him see the action, etc. If either you or your student can think of picturesque comparisons, share them. Also, look and listen for them in other stories, poems, etc.

Art: Musical Instruments - Banjo

In past *Five in a Row* stories of pioneer and mountain life you have seen different musical instruments that were popular. There have been guitars, fiddles (violins), dulcimers and now a banjo. Look at the picture on the last page and ask your student if he has ever seen or heard a banjo. Show your student a picture of a banjo, or watch a video of someone playing this instrument to let him hear the unique banjo sounds.

Notice how the last illustration of the story shows the joy released in the music and in celebrating together the triumph over an oppressing time. You might even ponder, with your student, what the Ward family might have been singing. Then you and your student can have a time of singing and dancing together!

(**Teacher's Note:** The banjo is a five-stringed instrument with a round body and a long neck. The body of the instrument is a small drum with a tightly stretched skin on one side. It is played very much like a guitar. Banjos were brought to North America by black slaves from Africa. Banjo music is often associated with the south, with jazz bands and with folk and country music. If you've completed FIAR, Vol. 1 and 2, your student can try the Musical Instrument Review at the end of this unit.)

Art: Imagination and Facial Expression

Discuss imagination with your student. We use it all the time. We imagine how we will look in a certain outfit we see at the store. We imagine what could be in the box we've received as a gift. Ask your student about the scene where Betsy Ward imagines something. What does she "see"? (She imagines the sheep as warm clothes for her children.) Do you think the illustrator, Helen Cogancherry, did a good job in putting into a picture what Betsy Ward is imagining?

You might also talk about the way the illustrator pictures the worry and the "wearing down" oppressive aspect on the features of Betsy Ward and her cold family. The first full-page picture of the story, opposite the little log cabin, shows their sad and somber faces. From the look on their faces, you can tell that the cold makes it hard just to get through each day. The next page also shows a worry and concern on the face of the mother (but maybe also a touch of "I will not give up" determination).

The children are definitely suffering from the cold and you can see it on their faces. Has your student ever been aware of the suffering of others because of the expressions he has seen on someone's face? **Compassion** (caring for the hurts of others) often begins when we become aware of other people's suffering through various clues, such as facial expressions.

Math: Subtraction and Addition

Betsy Ward buys eight sheep from the drover. Make up subtraction problems using scenarios from the text of the story: Two of the sheep are killed by wolves. How many are left alive? Then one of the sheep eats poisonweed and dies, leaving how many? Another sheep drowns in the creek and another breaks its leg, etc. Only three sheep are still alive the following spring. Because one is a ewe (YOU)—a female sheep, the Wards can raise more. Their ewe has lambs and the herd continues to increase. Lambs often give birth to twins. Make some addition problems from the "increase."

Science: Sheep

The sheep pictured in *Warm As Wool* have horns shaped much like those of Dorsets or Merinos, though the sheep in the story are not identified specifically. If you have access, visit a sheep farm, especially at spring shearing time. Enjoy the sheep shearing, and the lambs leaping about. If this is not possible, try to obtain some raw wool from a spinner, weaver, or a yarn shop. Let your student see how dirty it is if it has not been cleaned, and feel and smell the oily lanolin in the wool. (This is where we get lanolin, a skin softening ingredient used in many lotions and other products.)

Discuss the enemies of sheep, beginning with the ones you read about in *Warm as Wool*. (Wolves, poisonweed, deep water which weighs down the wool and causes the animals to drown, and holes in the ground that can break legs.) Other enemies are foot rot and sore mouth, diseases that are common to sheep. They can have internal parasites and diseases spread by mites and ticks. In addition, predatory animals and dogs sometimes kill sheep.

Sheep have many symbolic meanings. Rams are often associated with power and strength, while lambs often symbolize innocence or gentleness. There are many important references to lambs and sheep in the Bible. And sheep have been the focus of stories like Odysseus' escape from the cave of the Cyclops (*The Odyssey*, by Homer) and nursery rhymes like *Mary Had a Little Lamb* and *Little Boy Blue*. You could make a list with your student of stories, poems, songs, etc., which mention sheep.

(**Teacher's Note:** The following is teacher information only, but it may provide an interesting avenue of study for you or your older student:)

Sheep are fascinating animals and have been important to humans for thousands of years. They are raised and herded in almost all parts of the world for their wool (fleece) and for their meat. There are so many facets of sheep and sheep-keeping that you could do a complete unit study with such topics as: the zoological aspects of sheep (800 different breeds with subtle differences; breeding; scientific classification; the fact they are cud chewers and they have split hooves, etc.), shearing, spinning and weaving, the historic place of sheep ranching in the Old West (and the battles with the cattle ranchers over the sheep ranchers' fences), largest sheep-producing countries (Australia, China, New Zealand), etc., the leading sheep-raising states, which are Texas, California, Colorado, etc. In fact, the ten leading sheep-raising states are all west of the Mississippi River. Sheep need lots of range over which to roam and graze.

There are vocabulary words connected with sheep, such as: flock, fleece, rams, ewes, lambs, domestic, breeds, cud, big horn, horns, wool, etc. Then there are the names of different breeds of sheep: Dorset, Merino, Lincoln, Cheviot, Romney, Suffolk, Karakul, Corridale, Rambouillet and many others. Some of these sheep have long wool, some fine wool and some have a coarse wool. Some have horns and some do not.

Teacher's Notes

The *Five in a Row* lesson options for each unit in the manual are all you need to teach your child. The additional resource area provided below is simply a place to jot down relevant info you've found that you might want to reference.

WARM AS WOOL

Date:

Student:

Five in a Row Lesson Topics Chosen:

Social Studies:

Language Arts:

Art:

Math:

Science:

Relevant Library Resources: Books, DVDs, Audio Books

Websites or Video Links:

Related Field Trip Opportunities:

Favorite Quote or Memory During Study:

Name:

Date:

Social Studies: **Covered Wagons**

Help your student measure out 15 feet by 4 feet on a floor or outside on the ground. Use painters tape or masking tape to mark the length and width on carpet or flooring. Use chalk if you are outside.

These measurements are the typical size of a covered wagon. Discuss again all the things that a family would need to have in that small space. If outside, your student may wish to draw items in their covered wagon with chalk.

Take a photo of your student inside the measured space and paste it into the frame below. Or your student can use the space below to draw their covered wagon, or how their chosen items would fit inside.

Musical Instrument Review

For FIAR Volumes 1, 2 and 3

Match the number beside each instrument with the story in which it appears:

Bagpipes Wee Gillis, Vol. 2 _____

Flute The Bee Tree, Vol. 3 _____

Banjo Warm as Wool, Vol. 3 _____

Violin Daniel's Duck, Vol. 3 _____

Harmonica Lentil, Vol. 1 and The Finest Horse in Town, Vol. 3 _____

Piano Babar, To Duet or Not to Duet, Vol. 2 _____

Dulcimer Daniel's Duck, Vol. 3 _____

Name:

Date:

Social Studies: **Geography and History**

With your student, make a map for his notebook that traces the trip Betsy and Josiah Ward's family made in 1803 from Connecticut to Ohio. Be sure to include wagoning through New York State, crossing Lake Erie and landing near Cleveland with as many illustrations and labels as you like. You could work on this project for a short time each day during the week.

150

Connecticut

Ohio

The Salamander Room

Title:	*The Salamander Room*
Author:	Anne Mazer
Illustrator:	Steve Johnson and Lou Fancher
Copyright:	1991
Award:	Reading Rainbow Selection
Summary:	For those who have always wished they could bring all the outside indoors— an imaginative conversation between a nature lover and his mother.

Social Studies: Relationships - Mother and Child

In this story, a mother asks her son questions about his plans to care for a wild creature. There is an intimacy between them as the mother continues to listen and allows her son to create an imaginary world that he wishes "could be."

Does your student share special interests and secret imaginings with her mother? Do you have any "flights of fancy" (things that you wished for that were rather fantastic) that you can remember from your childhood to share with your student?

Language Arts: List Making

Make an illustrated list with your young student of all the things Brian thought of to make a nice home for his salamander: fresh green leaves, shiny wet leaves, moss, crickets, bull frogs, water, tree stumps, boulders, salamander friends, insects and bugs, waterpools, birds, trees, ponds, rain, sun, vines, ferns, mushrooms, stars, moon and owls.

Looking at the list, let your student compose and draw her own picture of a salamander room. Encourage her to add anything else she can think of that would please the red-orange pet.

Language Arts: Setting

The setting of the story opens in the woods where Brian finds his red-orange salamander. The setting then shifts to Brian's room which slowly, through his imaginative ideas, begins to turn back into the woods again. You might want to discuss with your student the fact that this is an unusual and creative way to treat the story setting.

Maybe she would like to try a story that begins with a certain setting; the setting shifts and then returns to the original setting. The story may be imaginative or it can be more realistic. It could begin in a child's room with the child going outside or taking a trip and then returning to the room to change her clothes or write the events in a diary, etc. The idea is to include details of the original setting, change the place, have many new details and then return to some of the original setting's details once again. Brian's pet salamander might be found in anywhere in the eastern United States, so place the story disk on any state that your student chooses.

Language Arts: Parallel Construction

Very simply speaking, parallel construction means the same thing on both sides, like balance. This story has a type of parallel construction because each conversation has a "mother side" and a "son side." The replies are not necessarily even, but the mother's question is, in each case, balanced by the son's reply. If you decide to introduce this concept to your young student, you might get a balance scale or draw one and say, "let's look and see if each conversation is parallel or balanced. Let's see if each conversation has a mother part and a son part." Put a penny on the scale or drawing when you read the mother's question, and a penny on the other side when you find the son's reply. This will graphically show the balance and the "parallelism." Ask your student if she thinks each of the mother's questions will be balanced in this way. Then, check it out together.

Your older student may want to try writing a similar type of story with parallel or balanced questions and answers.

Language Arts: Reading for Knowledge

Discuss with your student that one often reads books for pleasure, but sometimes a person simply needs information to answer particular questions. That's when she finds books on a certain topic and reads specifically for the knowledge and information to answer the question. Ask your student if she noticed Brian doing this.

The picture opposite the text: "He will miss his friends," shows a book. What do you think the book is? What kind of pictures does it have? Study it carefully and then look at the picture that goes with the text: "But the trees, how will they grow?" The scene is almost the same as the scene in Brian's book: the mushroom with the leaf over it. Look at the picture opposite the text: "The insects will multiply, and soon there will be bugs everywhere." In this picture, the book is now closed on the window seat, but open again upon the dresser of the next page. Brian has been reading up on the ideal living quarters for salamanders and possibly finding the answers for his mother's questions.

If you've read *Andy and the Lion*, you'll remember that Andy went to the library for a book on lions and learned a lot about them. Also, *Henry the Castaway* had read a great deal about exploring and things like the Orinoco River. Even Mary Ellen, in *The Bee Tree*, learned that when you must search for something in a book the reward is generally sweet. (These three books are all in this volume of FIAR.)

Art: Review

If you have completed Vol. 1 and 2 of *Five in a Row*, you could look for the following as a review: An example of **viewpoint** (first picture of Brian finding the salamander, where the picture looks up at Brian from a small creature's viewpoint), **shadows** (among others, notice the cover picture), **elongated circles, drawing trees, color palette, realistic artwork**, and though it isn't true **personification**, the salamander almost has a personality as it stares out the window and thinks about the forest.

Art: Use of Space and Dew Drops

Together with your student, notice how the artist has used the white frame around the picture of Brian's room. What happens to the white picture borders as you turn the pages? (Little by little, first a tree stump, then a boulder, encroach on the white border until eventually there is no white left in the picture. Brian is now sleeping in the woods!)

Also, look at the dew drop on the mushroom, the elongated circle shape and the white of the mushroom showing through. For a serious art student, find *Drawing from Nature* by Jim Arnosky, a good resource book which will give you and your student more ideas for your sketchbooks. Take it with you on a nature sketching outing some warm afternoon.

Math: Counting

Your young student may have fun hunting for creatures throughout the story to count. They are hidden everywhere, making it quite a game to seek them out and count at the same time!

Science: Love of Nature

Childhood is a great time to begin developing an interest in nature. There is a wonderful variety of insects, birds and creatures around, even in the city. If your student is not naturally inquisitive about the things of nature, begin to point out interesting details, asking "Have you ever seen such a small bug?" "Have you ever seen the sky so gray?" "Look! I found three different sizes of acorns." "Those clouds are different than I've seen recently," or "Can you believe that sunset?" and "Feel the rough bark on this tree!" Awakening your student to the wonders all around her is an especially enjoyable task for a teacher. (The illustration opposite the first page of text is the "face" of the joy and wonder of discovery! Look for other pictures showing Brian's face of wonder.)

Look with your student at the variety of insects, animal creatures and vegetation that are illustrated in *The Salamander Room*. You may just want to appreciate the intricacy of wings, colors and textures or you may want to find an identification guide and see if you can name some of the insects. Let your student tell you if she's seen a (woolly bear) caterpillar, a frog, or a dragonfly, etc. On outdoor explorations, see if you can find these creatures on the ground, on plants and in the air!

Each creature or plant is a marvel in itself. Each has many facets to discover and so much to appreciate and wonder about. (A third or fourth grade student might like to begin a nature journal where she records new birds, insects, cloud formations, etc., that she notices and identifies. These lists can be lifelong lists for those dedicated nature lovers.) Seek out a copy of *Secrets of a Wildlife Watcher* by Jim Arnosky. A treasure for a young nature lover, this book contains lots of information and also has a beginning journaling section in the back.

Remember that there are inveterate nature lovers, so you may have a student who will watch a bee for twenty minutes, stop at every blossom for a sniff and admire each drop of dew (even noticing that the garden looks upside down in the dewdrop!) Enjoy your nature-lover student and have as many outings and good books, etc. for her as you can to encourage and satisfy her thirst for the outdoors. You might also have a student who never seems to notice any of these things, and indeed she may never be as thrilled. Still, she can develop some understanding and appreciation for creation, with your guidance and encouragement.

Science: Scavenger Hunt

A scavenger hunt is an enjoyable and sometimes hilarious way to introduce different types of subjects. In this case, use it to help your student develop an "eye" for nature.

154

Give your student a list of items to be found and a grocery bag in which to gather the items, along with small, clear, plastic canisters for specimens (prescription or vitamin bottles, food containers or empty paint jars with holes punched in the tops make good options). Also, give her a pencil and pad of paper to record sightings. Take her outdoors and see what she can find. The list will have to be adjusted for the geographic area in which you teach and the climate. Below is a sample list:

Scavenger Hunt - Time Limit: 20 Minutes

> 5 different insects
> 2 butterfly sightings
> 1 cicada or its shell
> 5 leaves from different trees
> 2 different colored rocks
> 3 flower sightings
> 4 bird sightings
> 1 spider web sighting
> 1 bird nest sighting
> 1 ant hill sighting

You may want to do the scavenger hunt with your young student and let your older student try it on her own. Remember to exercise safety around bees, wasps and spiders. This might also be a good time to talk about poison ivy, ticks and other hazards in your particular area.

If you're able to find this extra book, then you can snuggle up after your scavenger hunt with *Crinkleroot's Guide to Walking in Wild Places* by Jim Arnosky. In this book you'll read about another nature walk and enjoy lots of illustrations from nature. Maybe it will inspire a future outing!

(**Teacher's Note:** There are several other Crinkleroot

books that you may be able to locate online. They are worth the search for your student who loves nature!)

Science: Salamanders

Salamanders, like the one Brian found in the woods, live under rocks, logs and sometime in caves where it is moist, dark and cool. Salamanders are **amphibians**, like frogs, toads and newts. These animals begin life as a egg in the water. They hatch into a larval state and breathe underwater by means of gills. As they mature they develop legs and most develop lungs. Then they become land animals. The fact that they begin in the water and later live on land is the reason for their name "amphibian," which comes from the Greek word *amphibios*, meaning double life.

At the end of this unit, you will find a page of the life cycle of a salamander. You might want to just show your student the page and discuss it. You could also cut it apart, place each developmental stage on an index card, mix up the cards and let your student put them in proper order explaining the life cycle of a salamander.

Science: Crickets

Many insects are shown in the drawings of *The Salamander Room*. At almost any pond you may see most of these. The first illustration of this story shows crickets on Brian's nightstand. Male crickets make the musical songs of night-time. Your student might be inspired to find a cricket to keep for a few days, as is often done in China and Japan. (Remember, if you want to hear it **sing**, you have to find a **male cricket**. These are easily identified as the female has a long ovipositor and the male does not. Find some crickets and let your student see the difference.)

You can identify a female cricket by her egg-laying ovipositer. The female cricket does **not** sing.

The story *A Pocketful of Cricket* by Rebecca Caudill tells of a boy's pet cricket and the special ways he cares for it. This would be a good follow-up book for *The Salamander Room*. For a read-aloud book try *The Cricket In Times Square* by George Selden. And don't forget Jiminy Cricket in the Walt Disney movie classic, *Pinocchio*.

Science: Butterflies

Find a reference book for the butterflies of your area and brush up on the common names so that when your student spots one you can quickly iden-tify it. If there is an area where you could grow some parsley, put in several plants. During the summer, watch the plants for a green and yellow striped caterpillar. This is the larval stage of a swallowtail butterfly. When you find a caterpillar on the parsley, break off a bunch and place it in a small glass of water along with a simple stick. The water will keep the parsley fresh and the stick is where the caterpillar will make its chrysalis (KRIS-uh-lis). Place the glass with the parsley in another bowl of water to keep your caterpillar from "escaping" into your house. The caterpillar will eat the parsley. You may have to replace it several times, but eventually it will form a chrysalis on the stick where it will change body shapes by a process called metamorphosis (met-a-MORE-fuh-sis) into a swallowtail butterfly. One day you'll find the butterfly flying about your house! Enjoy the excitement. Then carefully let the butterfly

outdoors. There are many specific herbs, flowers and shrubs which you can plant to draw butterflies if you or your student has an interest in them.

Science: Classification of the Animal Kingdom - Vertebrates

(**Teacher's Note:** *This information is extremely advanced for young students and is included for your convenience.* In keeping with the Five in a Row tradition, you may decide to present tiny pieces of information with lots of pictures, in an informal way, just to introduce the concepts for the first time. Memorization is not the point of this exercise. You decide if you think it's appropriate to introduce a few of these concepts and let your student hear the vocabulary and create a base on which to build in the future. It helps to keep a teacher's file for each subject, science, English, history, etc., to let you know from year to year what you have previously introduced, and from what point you wish to continue.)

Two of the major groupings of the animal kingdom are the **invertebrates** (in-VERT-uh-brits)—animals without backbones, and the **vertebrates** (VERT-uh-brits)—animals with backbones.

Invertebrates include one-celled protozoa (like amoebas), sponges, flat worms, mollusks (like clams), arthropoda (insects, spiders, lobsters, etc.), echinoderms (like starfish), and other phylum groupings. The butterflies and bugs shown in *The Salamander Room* are all invertebrates.

Vertebrates are divided into classes: mammals, reptiles, amphibians, birds and fish (technically there are three classes of fish but that is too advanced for this introduction).

Here is a suggestion for a brief introduction to vertebrates: use a plastic index card box that holds 4x6 index cards. For the study of vertebrates, take each card and find or draw a picture for each of the five classes. On each card, put one of the five pictures to one side. Use a marker to write the name of the class of vertebrate and note the main characteristics of that group on the front or back of the card:

Mammals are warm-blooded, have a backbone, usually have hair and produce milk for their young. Humans are mammals, and so are dogs, whales, elephants and horses.

Amphibians are cold-blooded, have a backbone, and usually have moist skin without scales. Frogs, newts, salamanders and toads are amphibians. Amphibians lay their eggs in water, the eggs hatch and a usually a larva stage is reached where the young have gills and breathe under water. Later, legs and lungs develop in most species.

Reptiles are cold-blooded animals with a backbone. They breathe by lungs and usually have skin covered with plates or scales. Snakes, turtles, lizards, alligators and crocodiles are reptiles.

Birds are animals that have wings, feathers, two legs and a beak or bill. Birds are warm-blooded, have backbones and lay eggs.

Fish are cold-blooded animals with a backbone that live in water, breathe through gills, are covered with scales, and often have fins to help them swim. Some fish lay eggs and some are live bearers.

These illustrated cards will be a ready reference for review, and someday can be paired with the cards of the invertebrates for the overview of the entire animal kingdom.

As your student progresses through school and reads about different animals in books, ask her from time to time to what class of vertebrates does that animal belong. Or when taking walks, the animals that you and your student discover and see can be classified now and then in their own particular groups. (For upper-grade students, you can even break the mammals into orders, i.e., **rodents** (squirrels, mice, gophers, etc.), **marsupials** (opossums, kangaroos, etc.), **primates** (monkeys, gorillas, chimpanzees, etc.) and others. Take a trip to a pet store or zoo and have fun finding as many types of vertebrates as you can and deciding to which class each belongs. (Remember in a pet store to point out that a tarantula or cricket, etc., are not vertebrates.)

You can make a game with a package or two of 3x5" index cards. Use pictures of many different animals from all five classes of vertebrates. Glue one picture to a card. Let your student mix them up and then sort them out into the right groups. You can use clean styrofoam meat trays labeled Mammals, Birds, etc. and sort the cards right into the trays.

The game can become more detailed (at higher grade levels) as the first two trays are labeled: *Vertebrates* and *Invertebrates*. After sorting the cards (which now include cards with a spider, an amoeba, a clam, and other invertebrates) into two piles, vertebrates or invertebrates, each pile can be picked up and resorted into their respective classes. (If you have junior high or higher grade levels at home too, you can add the "scientific" class name to the tray. For instance the sorting tray labeled "Birds" can now also say "Aves," and the tray labeled "Fish", "Osteichthyes." Others are Mammalia, Reptilia, and Amphibia.

Teacher's Note: If you've used *Before FIAR, 2nd Edition* or *More Before FIAR* you will have a large collection of animal classification cards to use for this game. If not, you can find pictures of animals and insects online or in wildlife magazines. Search online for your state's department of convservation and see if they offer any free resources for kids (or homeschoolers). Many offer a kids wildlife magazine with pictures and articles based on local wildlife!

Teacher's Notes

The *Five in a Row* lesson options for each unit in the manual are all you need to teach your child. The additional resource area provided below is simply a place to jot down relevant info you've found that you might want to reference.

THE SALAMANDER ROOM

Date: _____

Student: _____

Five in a Row Lesson Topics Chosen:

Social Studies:
_____
_____
_____

Language Arts:
_____
_____
_____

Art:
_____
_____
_____

Math:
_____
_____
_____

Science:
_____
_____
_____

Relevant Library Resources: Books, DVDs, Audio Books

_____
_____
_____
_____
_____
_____
_____

Websites or Video Links:

_____
_____
_____
_____
_____
_____

Related Field Trip Opportunities:
_____
_____
_____

Favorite Quote or Memory During Study:
_____
_____
_____

160

Amphibious Life Cycles

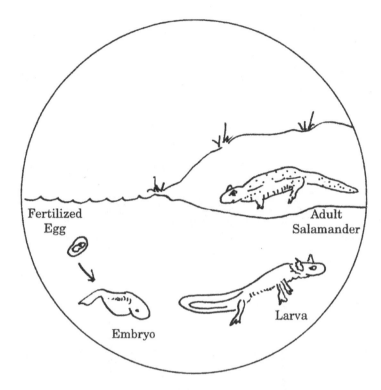

Salamanders

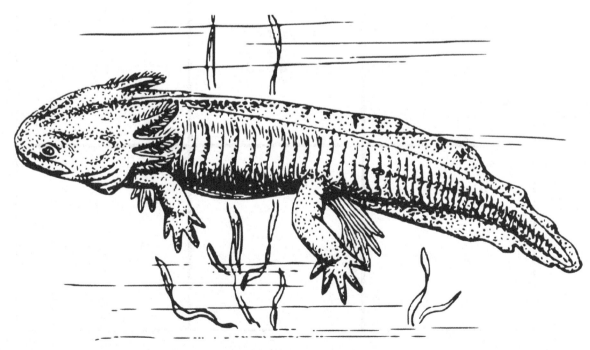

Larva

Name:

Date:

Science: **Nature Bingo**

In addition to the scavenger hunt idea in the manual, you can enjoy a game of Nature Bingo. Copy this page then write or draw nature items that are local to your area into the squares on the bingo card. See if you can get 3 squares in a row with things you see or collect on a nature walk or even in your own backyard. *Examples:* birds, buterflies, leaves, bugs, spiders, etc.

NATURE BINGO		
	FREE	

Name:

Date:

Language Arts: **List Making**

Make an illustrated list with your young student of all the things Brian thought of to make a nice home for his salamander: fresh green leaves, shiny wet leaves, moss, crickets, bull frogs, water, tree stumps, boulders, salamander friends, insects and bugs, waterpools, birds, trees, ponds, rain, sun, vines, ferns, mushrooms, stars, moon and owls.

Looking at the list, let your student compose and draw his own picture of a salamander room in the space below. Encourage him to add anything else he can think of that would please the red-orange pet.

Climbing Kansas Mountains

Title:	*Climbing Kansas Mountains*
Author:	George Shannon
Illustrator:	Thomas B. Allen
Copyright:	1993
Summary:	A father and son share a special outing on a mountain of a metaphor!

Social Studies: United States Geography - Kansas

Kansas is in the central part of the United States in what is called the Midwest. It is a part of the Great Plains that nestle between the Mississippi River and the Rocky Mountains. Kansas is, as you can tell from the story, a relatively flat state with a climate right for growing great amounts of wheat, corn and other food products. While traveling across Kansas you may see large signs on the edges of farms that tell how many thousand people can be fed from the grain produced on each farm.

Although there are some larger cities in Kansas, this story seems to take place in a small farm town. The tiny park and Uncle Roy's Cafe and the grain elevators are clues to a *small* Kansas *farm* town. A city would probably have a large park and perhaps fancier restaurants.

Did you notice that Sam speaks of *Uncle* Roy's Cafe but the sign only says Roy's Cafe, making it a good guess that Roy really is Sam's uncle!

Place your story disk on Kansas.

Social Studies: State Symbols

Most states have a designated state bird, state tree and state flower. In *Climbing Kansas Mountains* the illustrator chose to include the state bird of Kansas (a meadowlark on the dedication page) and the Kansas state flower (a sunflower on the back cover). The Kansas state tree is the cottonwood and though you can't tell exactly, there may have been some cottonwoods in the tall trees in town.

Your older student may want to look online or in a library book about Kansas to learn more about this state and also research the state symbol, seal and flag.

If you think it appropriate, you could suggest that your student research and find his own state symbols, and make a page for his notebook with drawn and labeled symbols.

Social Studies: Relationship - Father and Son

What a kind father to see that his son needed a little "one on one" time! What fun for Sam to go alone with his father on a secret adventure. Sam's father is making a memory, and when they reach the grain elevators and climb to the top, they don't say a word. Why? (Because it is an inspiring sight and it takes a while just to gaze at the height and the magnificence before they can think of anything to say. This is very like the experience the father and child have in *Owl Moon* when they are staring at the owl. In *Owl Moon*, by Jane Yolen (FIAR Vol. 2) the child says, " ...when you go owling, you don't need words.")

Another aspect of relationships is making choices. Sam's father allows him to make a choice. Sam can decide for himself whether or not he wants to go on the outing. Sam can't imagine how his father can be talking about mountains (especially after making the map!), but he takes a chance and goes with him anyway. Many of our experiences consist of making choices and taking chances, not knowing if we'll really enjoy something or not. Sometimes it works out and sometimes it doesn't, but choices and chances are part of the variety of life.

Sam also experiences a close feeling with his father in the "Got you!, Got me!" type of joking together and the way Sam uses a favorite phrase of his father's, "when pigs fly." The father also agrees with Sam's metaphor of the fields being a table and they enjoy that imagery together.

Social Studies: Occupation - Grain Handlers

Many men and women earn their living by producing wheat, corn, soybeans and other grains. In the case of Kansas wheat, some of those occupations might include:

Farmers: These are the men and women who actually work the fields, plowing, planting, fertilizing, etc. Some farmers own their land and others only rent it. Farmers can work as little as 5 or 10 acres or as many as 5,000 or 10,000.

Combine crews: Sometimes farmers harvest their own wheat in Kansas, but many farmers hire "custom combining crews" who travel slowly northward during summer and fall, harvesting the wheat fields for money. These crews own very expensive, large combines (COM-bines) and trucks. They help get the wheat in quickly during harvest time.

Grain elevator operators: Once the wheat is harvested, it is stored in grain elevators. Some farmers own their own storage silos, but most deliver their grain to an area elevator operator who weighs and carefully stores the wheat in enormous towers until the farmer sells his wheat and ships it out.

Truckers: Much of the wheat sold by farmers is hauled by trailer to market. During harvest season, many truck drivers stay busy hauling the wheat harvest to market in their trailers.

Railroad workers: The majority of grain is shipped by rail. Railroad crews stay busy during harvest, pulling long strings of grain hopper cars filled with wheat. It's not uncommon to see more than 120 cars full of wheat on one train, trailing more than one and a half miles behind the locomotive!

Merchant Marine ship crews: Much of the grain produced in the United States and Canada is sold and shipped to other nations worldwide. Kansas wheat is loaded on rail cars or river barges and sent to either the Great Lakes or the Gulf of Mexico where it is loaded on enormous cargo ships larger than football fields and shipped to countries around the world.

Perhaps your older student would like to draw a picture of one or more of these groups of people. Or, he could design a long "mural" on a roll of butcher paper, illustrating each of the many people who handle the grain between the farm and the consumer.

Some students might enjoy acting out one or more of the roles, pretending to be a train engineer, truck driver or custom combiner.

Language Arts: Good Descriptive Writing

For your older student, talk about writing good descriptive phrases. Such phrases often bring a picture to mind or give special information. In *Climbing Kansas Mountains* there is an abundance of descriptive phrases.

For example, as Sam and his father pass the park, the author writes about a school with a broken slide. This immediately paints a picture in one's mind, and the joy of a special detail rather than just "we passed the school." Another example is "the old yellow house where I learned to walk." The author is putting in details about the house; it was old and yellow. He's also including details about Sam: the yellow house was where he learned to walk. These kind of details make the story much more interesting. It gives the reader the feeling that he knows something special about Sam's life.

Have your young student try dictating a story about himself, putting in some interesting details. Your older student can try a similar story while you gently encourage him to include descriptive phrases and interesting details.

Language Arts:
Poetic Device - Simile and Metaphor

If you have studied Vol. 1 and 2 of FIAR, the concept of **simile** and **metaphor** will not be new for your student. The interesting thing about *Climbing Kansas Mountains* is that the entire idea of the story is a metaphor. The "Kansas mountains" are not mountains at all; they are really grain elevators! And the table that is so big it has no edge, with a green centerpiece is actually the vast plowed squares of field, with the trees in town at the center.

Teacher's Note: If you have not studied Vol. 1 and 2, similes and metaphors are comparisons. They compare two unlike things, and similes use words of comparison: like, as, seems, etc. His hair was *like* ripened wheat. Fields that looked *like* corduroy. Metaphors make a similar comparison but go further, calling one thing another; the grain elevators *are* Kansas mountains (not just "like"). For additional examples and writing suggestions, refer to FIAR Vol. 1 and 2.

Ask your student if he hears examples of similes while reading *Climbing Kansas Mountains*. Some he might notice are: *like* a sneaky cat, smooth *as* fancy pants, field squares plowed up *like* corduroy.

Language Arts: Memory Details

As a short memory exercise, ask your student some questions: Does the story mention Sam's sisters, brothers or both? (brothers) What kind of Kansas map did Sam's father help him make? (flour dough) On what day of the week did the special mountain adventure happen? (Sunday) Maybe your student would like to quiz you on a question or two.

Art: Mixed Medium - Pastels, Charcoal and Colored Pencils

Thomas B. Allen, the artist that illustrated *Climbing Kansas Mountains*, has used a mixed medium for the pictures. Your student can easily see the rough texture of the paper under the chalk colors, and the faint charcoal or colored pencil outline around the figures. Your inquisitive art student could carefully search the pictures for the different areas of pastel chalk, charcoal or colored pencil.

Notice Sam's head in the car as they pass Roy's Cafe. It is down low; he is young. Turn the page quickly and see how tall the father is. These two pictures together hint at Sam's youth.

Also, the artist has drawn Sam standing in a Kansas wheat field, with hair that looks exactly like the wheat!

Art: Symbolism

The last illustration of the story shows a tablecloth with centerpiece superimposed on the wheat fields and the grain elevator in the distance. There is symbolism in this illustration because the Midwest (of which Kansas is a part) is also known as the "Bread Basket" of America. This is because of the amount of wheat grown there and the food products that are made from the wheat. There is a very good chance that the bread that appears on your student's table came from wheat grown in Kansas. So the table, over the fields, is symbolic of "feeding the nation." Drawing pictures that show ideas in a symbolic way is one choice that an artist can make. If you are compiling a list of Choices an Artist Can Make, add the question "Do I want to show any symbolism in my picture?"

One of the comparisons that Sam makes is that the roads look like the red ribbon stripes in the tablecloth. Ask your student to study the picture carefully and notice the different items on the table. Does he notice the car driving its way across the ribbon roads?

Art: Flour Dough Map

If you think it would be fun, make a flour dough map of the state in which your student lives. One way you could begin, is to tape a large sheet of plain paper to a piece of strong cardboard. Then find a good map that shows the relief (indicating hills and valleys) of the state. Begin by hand-drawing the shape of the state, and enlarging it to fit your paper. Don't worry if it's not absolutely perfect, the dough is forgiving! Let your student do as much as he can.

Mix equal parts of flour and salt and moisten with water to "Play-Doh® consistency." Knead the dough until soft and then pat over the board, moving up to the outer lines of the hand drawn map. Use extra dough or pinch up areas of dough where any mountains or hills exist and add any other geographic features of your area.

If your student lives in an area with hills or mountains, it might be interesting for him to also make a small map of Kansas and see for himself that it is relatively flat land with "hardly a bump." If your student's state is rather flat, remind him that it is like Kansas. Maybe he would like to try a small map of a state that has mountains, so he can "see" the difference between the mountainous state and his state.

With your older student: if you are gaining a lot of geographic understanding with dough map making and having a lot of fun, you might want to consider a cookie sheet size map of the United States. This project could reveal many concepts about the two major mountain ranges, and the Great Plains watershed to the Mississippi, etc. These ideas can be discovered by your student in the actual making of the map., You can help by asking just a few leading questions, i.e., "If it rains over the Rocky Mountains, where will the water go?"

The answer that your student will be able to see, perhaps even for himself, is the water will divide and some will flow down the west side of the mountains, toward the Pacific Ocean, and some will flow down the east side of the mountains, eventually to the Mississippi River. You may want to mention the Continental Divide, Great Salt Lake, the Grand Canyon and Colorado River, the Great Lakes, etc., especially if any of these are in your student's vacation plans!

Math: Adding and Multiplying

The grain elevators were "as tall as eight houses stacked." This is a wonderful opportunity to explore both addition and multiplication. Young students can use cut-out pictures, or draw simple houses and cut them out to count to eight. Older students might want to estimate the actual height of the grain elevators by multiplying the typical height of a house times eight. (One-story houses are typically 10-12 feet high, while two-story houses are 20-24 feet high.)

Math: Acres

Farm fields are measured in acres. One acre is 4,840 square yards, which is approximately the same size as a football field. Most city homes have yards between 1/4 and 1/2 acre in size. Large suburban homes might have a yard from 1/2 to 1 acre. Wheat farms in Kansas are measured in hundreds, or even thousands of acres. 640 acres of land is called a section of land. It is one mile by one mile in size. Imagine how big a 6,400 acre Kansas wheat farm would be! It could be a mile long and ten miles wide, or more than three miles on each side! Just discussing the concept of an acre with your older student will begin to familiarize him with this common land measurement.

Math: Grain Measurements

Grain is measured in bushels. If you have a bushel basket available, show your student what a bushel looks like. Farmers discuss how many "bushels per acre" their crops produce. Perhaps a successful farmer might get 100 bushels of grain from one acre of his farm. A bushel measure is also 4 pecks, 8 gallons or 32 quarts. You could show your student a quart container and a gallon milk jug and talk about how many times you'd have to fill each of these to have a bushel. If you'd like, try measuring how many quarts of water it takes to fill a gallon (4) and then how much 8 gallons looks like when poured into a large plastic wastebasket, washtub or trash can. Pick a warm day and go outside and have the wettest math lesson of the year!

Acquire some wheat grains and let your younger student count the number in a tablespoon. By adding or measuring, your older student could find the number of tablespoons in a whole cup (16) and from there, a quart and a bushel. Now, he can multiply times the number of grains per tablespoon. Your older student will be amazed at how many grains of wheat are in a bushel. For your oldest students, let them try multiplying the number of grains in a bushel times 100 bushels per acre, times, say, a 1,000 acre farm! That's how many wheat grains a typical Kansas wheat farmer might grow in a season!

Science: Botany - The Grain of Wheat

Even your young student may be aware of the terms "wheat flour" or bran, like in bran muffins, or wheat germ that he may have had on cereal. The wheat kernel has an outer husk, under which is a bran covering with the endosperm next. The wheat germ is much smaller and near the center. Try to find a stalk of wheat, preferably from a field, or perhaps at a store (sometimes craft stores). Let your student examine each different part.

Also, hold one grain of wheat in your hand and find the picture of the grain elevator beside the railroad tracks in the story. Look at the wheat grain and try to imagine how many it would take to fill a building nine stories high!

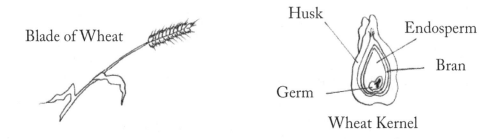

Blade of Wheat

Husk
Endosperm
Bran
Germ
Wheat Kernel

Sprout some wheat and watch it grow, or look for a wheat field nearby, if possible, to watch through the growing and harvesting cycle.

For your older student, have him research **winter wheat** (grown in mild climates) and **spring wheat** (grown in cold winter climates), as well as hard and soft varieties of wheat.

If you have not already read *The King of Prussia and the Peanut Butter Sandwich*, by Alice Fleming, this story would fit perfectly with the subject of wheat. Your older student will *love* this amazing story of persevering children handling a big responsibility. And he'll learn how their work affected their lives and ours!

Science: Wheat to Flour to Bread

Leading wheat-producing states and Canadian provinces include: Kansas, North Dakota, Washington, Oklahoma, Saskatchewan and Alberta. The top five wheat producing countries in the world are China, India, Russia, United States and France.

In order to use wheat grain, it must be cracked or ground. There are large flour mills that grind the grain into flour. In some countries grindstones are turned by water wheels or by windmills, and in others people still grind their grain by hand on stones. The ground grain is then combined with water to make bread. Some people have home grain mills that grind smaller amounts of flour for home use.

Make some bread and think about the view from "a Kansas mountain."

Science: What Is A Mountain?

Sam's father said what made a mountain was a high, quiet view. Mountains have a high view, and while some may be quiet, many mountains have wind blowing strongly at higher altitudes. This might make a high "loud" view!

The high view that "makes a mountain" is its **elevation above sea-level**. A mountain is a high hill that rises significantly above the surrounding area. Some mountains are thousands of feet high. Some are so high that the trees don't grow at the top (above the **timberline**) because it is so cold. Many have snow on them all year round.

Mountains have an endless list of topics that one can examine including the **plant and animal life** of certain mountains and mountain ranges, the **weather** at certain mountain locations, **historic travel** over the mountains, **songs** about mountains ("On Top of Old Smoky", "America the Beautiful", "She'll Be Comin' Round the Mountain", etc.) and **sayings** such as "don't make a mountain out of a mole hill" "it's a mountain top experience" or "that's a mountain of trouble." There are also wonderful **forms of recreation** available on the mountains such as camping, hiking, mountain climbing, rappelling and skiing.

Mountains can be exciting and interesting. Each mountain top "face" is different, stretching the imagination and giving ample subject material for expressive thoughts and writing. Your older student might enjoy learning about some of the highest and most famous mountains in the world, and where they are located:

Mt. Everest (Nepal-China border) ....29,028 ft.

Denali* (United States) ....20,320 ft.
    *formerly Mt. McKinley

Mt. Kilimanjaro (Tanzania) ....19,344 ft.

The Matterhorn (Italy-Switzerland border) 14,691 ft.

Mt. Fuji (Japan) ....2,388 ft.

Mt. Cook (New Zealand)............................12,349 ft.

Mt. Vesuvius (Italy) ....4,190 ft.

Teacher's Note: There are some mountains that fit between the above listings, but these are the most popular giants.

Many exciting stories have been written about people who wanted to climb or explore these mountains and Mt. Vesuvius certainly has its own fascinating story. Let your older student explore any of these topics that interest him.

Rand McNally's Picture Atlas of the World, illustrated by Brian Delf has wonderful maps that show mountains and ranges for each country's map, and a page of the highest mountains of the world stacked up together for a great graphic effect. This book is very helpful as a constant resource for teaching geography in an exciting way.

Teacher's Notes

The *Five in a Row* lesson options for each unit in the manual are all you need to teach your child. The additional resource area provided below is simply a place to jot down relevant info you've found that you might want to reference.

CLIMBING KANSAS MOUNTAINS

Date: _____

Student: _____

Five in a Row Lesson Topics Chosen:

Social Studies:
_____
_____
_____

Language Arts:
_____
_____
_____

Art:
_____
_____
_____

Math:
_____
_____
_____

Science:
_____
_____
_____

Relevant Library Resources: Books, DVDs, Audio Books

_____
_____
_____
_____
_____
_____
_____

Websites or Video Links:

_____
_____
_____
_____
_____
_____
_____
_____

Related Field Trip Opportunities:
_____
_____
_____

Favorite Quote or Memory During Study:
_____
_____
_____

172

Name:

Date:

Social Studies: **State Symbols**

Most states have a designated state bird, state tree and state flower. In *Climbing Kansas Mountains* the illustrator chose to include the state bird of Kansas (a meadowlark on the dedication page) and the Kansas state flower (a sunflower on the back cover). The Kansas state tree is the cottonwood and though you can't tell exactly, there may have been some cottonwoods in the tall trees in town.

Search online for photographs of a meadowlark, sunflower, and cottonwood tree. Print off the images or draw your own in the spaces provided.

| Meadowlark | Sunflower | Cottonwood Tree |

Notes for any other research about Kansas:

_____

_____

_____

_____

Name:

Date:

Geography: **Kansas Flag**

The flag of Kansas has a dark blue field with the state seal in the center.
Above the seal is a sunflower sitting over a stripe of gold and light blue.
Below the state seal, in large letters, is the word "KANSAS."
For more information, see Parts of a Flag on page 224.

Color in the Kansas flag below.

Name:

Date:

Science: **What is a Mountain?**

Mountains can be exciting and interesting. Each mountain top "face" is different, stretching the imagination and giving ample subject material for expressive thoughts and writing. Your older student might enjoy learning about some of the highest and most famous mountains in the world, and where they are located.

Spaces are provided below for you to paste printed pictures of 3 mountains from your research. You can list interesting facts you've learned below the photos.

Amber on the Mountain

Title: *Amber on the Mountain*

Author: Tony Johnston

Illustrator: Robert Duncan

Copyright: 1994

Summary: Ever wish you had a friend? Ever have to say good-bye to one? Amber receives the gift of reading from her new friend, and sends the gift of writing when her friend moves away.

Social Studies: Setting

We know from the title of the book and the illustrations that this book takes place somewhere on a mountain. After reading the book through, point out the tall mountain on the cover that is covered in snow, as well as the somewhat "pointy" mountains in many of the pictures inside. Illustrator Robert Duncan spent his childhood in Utah and Wyoming, two states in the Rocky Mountain region of North America. Tall, jagged, snow-covered mountains are common in the Rockies, so it's a safe bet that this area is a good one to place your story disk. Mountain culture is similar, though, to previous FIAR books you may have studied such as *Daniel's Duck* (Vol. 3), *Down Down the Mountain* (Vol. 2), or *The Rag Coat* (Vol. 1). Isolated areas are similar; there is much beauty, but loneliness is also a reality.

Social Studies: Character - Friendships

In the story *Andy and the Circus*, Andy is sociable and has lots of friends. But in *Amber on the Mountain*, Amber is shy and she lives where there are few children to be her friends. Discuss the difficulties of making friends when one is shy. If your student is shy, help her talk about her feelings. Because Amber is shy, she waits for just the right opportunity to meet Anna. Some people move slowly and carefully in all that they do. Each person is different, and that variety keeps life interesting. Encourage your student to appreciate the differences in the people she meets, rather than be impatient that they are not "just like her."

If your student is outgoing, then talk about helping people who are shy to feel comfortable and accepted. Sometimes a person who is shy needs gentle encouragement to be drawn into relationships. She needs to be invited for a visit or to an event. It is important for your student to know that not everyone is the same, or just like her. This is the beginning of teaching your student compassion and sensitivity to those around her.

Besides making friends or being friends, we often have to say good-bye to our friends. Talk with your student about the friendships each of you has made, and whether or not they were continued when separation occurred. Some friendships seem to last through anything and others sort of drift away. Discuss the inevitability of this fact of life.

In FIAR Vol. 1, there is a story called *Another Celebrated Dancing Bear* by Gladys Scheffrin-Falk in which one bear sees in his friend a desire to be a dancer, and sets about helping him fulfill that desire. One friend gives unselfishly to the other and both benefit. In *Amber On the Mountain*, Anna sees that Amber is embarrassed by not knowing how to read. Anna sees Amber's desire to learn. So Anna sets about helping Amber fulfill her dream. With your older student compare and contrast these two stories of real friends.

For your young student, ask if she remembers the story *Another Celebrated Dancing Bear* (reread it if you have it, or retell the story to each other). Then, ask your student if she can see how the stories are in any way the same. (Max is a good friend who really cares about Boris and his feelings. Anna is a good friend who really cares about Amber and her feelings. Max and Anna both give their time unselfishly. Both Max and Anna benefit from their giving, while Boris and Amber benefit from their friend's care. Both Boris and Amber have to work very hard to accomplish their goal, etc.)

Later, discuss differences. (Boris wants to learn to *dance* while Amber wants to learn to *read*, or Boris is *bored with his job* while Amber is *lonely* and thinks books can help the feeling of isolation, etc.) By gentle conversation, you are laying ground work for critical thinking and helping your student learn to compare and contrast ideas and characters.

Social Studies: Character - Successfully Handling Disappointment

Amber holds such high hopes to be able to read and write. The teacher who comes to her mountain almost brings Amber's hopes within reach. But the mountain life is so hard for the man. He leaves the mountain, delaying the fulfillment of Amber's dreams.

There is no mention of Amber being bitter or self-pitying. Maybe life in the mountains is so difficult that one gets used to disappointments. It's ironic that the very paper and pencils left after one disappointment are the same items she uses later to fulfill her dream of writing!

Can your student think of another disappointment for Amber besides the time her teacher leaves? (When her new friend Anna has to move.) It must have been very difficult for Amber to say good-bye when Anna had been such a good friend. Has your student ever had to say good-bye to someone she cared about? Do you have any special memories that you could share with her?

How did Amber handle this second disappointment?

(A possible clue to her feelings is found in the poem on the dedication page of *Amber On the Mountain*. The rain symbolizes the sad feelings of missing Anna, yet the poem ends with the joy of a letter which makes her seem close again. Reading between the lines of the story, Amber is extremely sad without Anna, but she continues to keep busy and one day decides to tackle the job of learning to write.)

Social Studies: Character - Determination & Accomplishments

Begin by asking your student the name of Amber's mule. (Rockhead) What does that name mean? Throughout this story, Amber speaks of being "rockheaded" like the mule. Normally, you would associate obstinate stubbornness with a mule, and indeed we often say "stubborn as a mule." But in this case, the proper shade of meaning for Anna and Amber's character was "determination." They were determined: Anna to teach, and Amber to learn. And they succeeded.

There was another man with determination in this story. Can your student think who it was? (Anna's father who said, "You can do almost anything you fix your mind on.") He set his mind on building the road and he succeeded, even though it was difficult. His influence through his daughter Anna helped Amber "set her mind" on learning to read. She, too, succeeded even though it was difficult.

Discuss setting goals and knowing the pleasure of accomplishment. Success takes work. Turn to the page with the two girls riding the horse together and reread the line, "Whatever else they did, every day they practiced reading." Continue talking about the day by day, persistent work that goes into reaching a goal and being successful. There is an old saying: "There is much drudgery between the first enthusiasm and the achievement." To overcome the drudgery of the day-by-day plodding along, one needs determination! (Remember the way Lentil practices his harmonica? *Lentil* by Robert McCloskey, FIAR Vol. 1.)

Social Studies: Mountain Culture

There is an entire subject to be explored in the traditions and ideas of the mountain people. (If you're interested in this topic, the Foxfire books are an excellent resource for high school or adult readers.) The unique, often isolated culture of mountain life sometimes leaves people out of touch with "modern ways." Granny, for example, exclaims, "You can't build a road here. Folks will roll clean off of it...." Her statement reflects the isolation of mountain life in days gone by. Ask your student why he thinks Granny believes this is true. (She has no knowledge of the engineering advances in road grading, etc., and it just doesn't seem possible to her.)

Another aspect to mountain culture is the unique music. Not everyone in the mountains could afford a banjo, guitar or fiddle so those who wanted to make music simply grabbed whatever was close at hand and enjoyed the pleasures of making music together. Gather up a bottle or jug to blow across, a grater or washboard to "run" with a spoon, spoons themselves (watch a video on how to play spoons: two spoons held back to back at the handle and slapped against the knee), whistles, bells, hair combs, etc. Enjoy a mountain music "jamboree." Play rhythms and sing traditional "mountain songs" such as *She'll Be Comin' Round the Mountain*, *Old Joe Clark* and *On Top of Old Smoky*. Now you have your own mountain music band!

Language Arts: Vocabulary

porcupine An animal with sharp quills, found in the woods.

skedaddle(d) Get out (leave) fast.

balk(ity) Stubbornly refuse to move; this is a creative adjective form.

slop The mixture of waste food fed to pigs.

pelter(ing) Strike or assail repeatedly; bombard (as by rain drops).

Language Arts: Poetic Devices - Simile

A simile is a comparison of two unlike things using connecting words such as "like," "as," etc. If your student has completed FIAR Vol. 1 and 2, she may point out a simile to you when she hears it. If not, you can talk about the first sentence of the book, which compares a mountain to a needle: " ... a mountain so

high, it poked through the clouds like a needle stuck in down." Does your student know that down is the soft under-feathers of geese or ducks, often made into feather beds or feather pillows? A pile of down (soft white feathers) would look something like clouds.

Other examples of simile:

*Amber and Anna stuck to each other **like** burrs.*

*Amber tangled the words **like** quilting thread.*

*The trees bristled **like** porcupine quills.*

*Her words came peltering thick **as** spring rain.*

*Clouds **like** grey geese.*

*Her tongue curled in concentration **like** a lizard stalking a bug.*

Your student might enjoy making some unusual comparisons herself. She could illustrate them and put them in her notebook. Check the Indexes of FIAR Vol. 1 and 2 for additional lessons on simile. There are many different illustrations and suggestions for writing assignments.

Language Arts: Parallelism

Amber On The Mountain has a beautifully poetic passage that also illustrates parallel construction:

"Mountain people went down the road and learned the ease of city ways. City people camp up the road and learned the beauty of mountain ways."

These sentence ideas run in a parallel word pattern and sound pleasing together as you read the paragraph. That is because there is a balance in the phrases. Notice that the mountain people are going down, while the city people are coming up. Also, the mountain people are learning city ways while the city people are learning mountain ways. The mountain people are passing the city people on parallel paths!

If your student would like, have her illustrate these sentence ideas in one picture. The mountain people could be passing the city people, with both going in opposite directions on the mountain! Even the idea of mountain beauty could be captured with flowers, pine trees, etc. on the mountain top, where the city dwellers were headed, and stores, etc., to show the city ways at the foot of the mountain where the mountain people were going.

Teacher's Note: The story *The Salamander Room* (in this volume) contains a lesson on parallel construction. In *The Salamander Room* each question of the mother is paralleled by the answer of the son. (Parallel means the construction of similar phrases or ideas on both sides—going along together, or in a balanced way.)

Art: Medium - Oil Paint

Robert Duncan used oil paint to illustrate *Amber On The Mountain*. In the first double-page picture at the beginning of the story, it is easy to see the build-up of paint in the yellow flowers and the brush strokes of the grass. These are clues for your student that oil has been used as the medium. (Acrylic paint can sometimes look this way too.)

Within a medium, the style of painting can vary greatly. In the illustrations for this story, Robert Duncan has chosen to use soft lines on the figures and objects which give an overall gentle effect to the pictures.

Art: Sculpture - Clay

When Amber and Anna had to say good-bye they gave each other parting gifts. Anna gave Amber the special book of fairy tales that had originally sparked their friendship. (It was the same book that Amber first read all by herself.)

Amber gave Anna a clay mule. Ask your student why she thinks Amber chose this gift. (Amber didn't have a lot of expensive things like books to give. The clay figure was a part of the mountain craft and mountain life, a good reminder for Anna. Probably Amber was thinking of how each of them had been "rockheaded" like Rockhead her mule, and how that determination had lead to such wonderful results. A clay mule would be just the right present to thank her "teacher" and friend, and remind her of their time together.)

For a sculpting project, using brown or gray clay, let your student fashion a mule in memory of Amber's good friendship. She may want to try her hand at other objects and figures, too. Your very young student might need some instruction. One way to make animal figures is to start with a piece of clay in a ball or roll for the torso. The legs and head can then be added as balls or rolls of clay and finally the features worked with pinching, and tools like a table knife, toothpick, metal nail file or sculptor's tools. If this project creates a great deal of interest in making clay figures, find good art books at the library or videos for further instruction.

Math: Counting

Amber on the Mountain is a story about learning to read. Ask your young student if she knows how many letters are in our English alphabet? If she doesn't know, write them out for her and let her count. She should count twenty-six letters. She can also count the number of months on a calendar to correspond with the part in the story where Anna leaves the mountain and the story says, "Months passed." Looking together at an actual calendar is a great way to familiarize your student with the months of the year; see the activty sheet at the end of this unit to record your student's learning for her notebook.

Science: Air At Higher Altitudes

This story begins with a description of the high mountain on which Amber lived. The author writes,

" ...the air made you giddy—it was that clear."

The high mountain air had a "thinner" atmosphere with less concentration of gases including oxygen. And of course an area of less population will definitely have less pollution. Therefore, the air is so clean and clear that it seems exhilarating!

(**Teacher's Note:** Most of the people of the world live in areas of 5,000 ft. altitude or less. The higher the altitude, the less atmospheric pressure and therefore, very simply, the less oxygen taken in by a body to the bloodstream. When a person does not get as much oxygen as they are used to, they may suffer dizziness, headache or nausea. People who live in the high Andes Mountains [as much as 22,000 feet high] or other high mountain regions become used to the lower levels of oxygen and are able to live more comfortably than those new to that environment.)

Science: Road Building

Granny thought the road could not be built. The man said it was possible. Maybe Granny thought he would try to build the road straight up the mountain. That would be too steep. Ask your student if she has ever noticed exactly how roads are often built in steep places. (Many times they curve around the hill or mountain slowly going higher at each round. The distance traveled is longer, but the descent and ascent is less radical.) If your student is interested, you can help her make a model of a mountain (out of clay or Play-Doh®). Cut in a spiraling road and talk about why roads are built this way. For an older student, give her the materials and challenge her to think of a way to build a safe road on a tall mountain and show you her ideas. Offer hints if needed!

The *Five in a Row* lesson options for each unit in the manual are all you need to teach your child. The additional resource area provided below is simply a place to jot down relevant info you've found that you might want to reference.

AMBER ON THE MOUNTAIN

Date:

Student:

Five in a Row Lesson Topics Chosen:

Social Studies:

_____

_____

_____

Language Arts:

_____

_____

_____

Art:

_____

_____

_____

Math:

_____

_____

_____

Science:

_____

_____

_____

**Relevant Library Resources:
Books, DVDs, Audio Books**

_____

_____

_____

_____

_____

_____

_____

_____

Websites or Video Links:

_____

_____

_____

_____

_____

_____

_____

_____

182

Related Field Trip Opportunities:

_____

_____

_____

Favorite Quote or Memory During Study:

_____

_____

_____

Name:

Date:

Math: **Counting**

Alphabet and Calendar Months

Ask your young student if she knows how many letters are in our English alphabet? She should count twenty-six letters. She can also count the number of months on a calendar to correspond with the part in the story where Anna leaves the mountain and the story says, "Months passed."

A B C D E F G H I J K L M
N O P Q R S T U V W X Y Z

Alphabet Total _____

Month Total _____

January	May	September
February	June	October
March	July	November
April	August	December

In addition to the lesson and hands-on modelling of a spiraling road around a play-dough mountain, use this sheet to discuss the word and definition of "switchback."

Switchback:

A zigzag road or trail used to climb a steep hill.

Virtual 🖥
FIELD TRIP

Lombard Street in San Francisco is famous for a one-block area with steep, hairpin (or switchback) turns.

Search "Lombard Street" online to find areal views or videos of this famous road.

Add a photo or drawing of Lombard Street in the space below.

Amber on the Mountain

Name:

Date:

Social Studies: **Setting Goals**

After reading *Amber on the Mountain* and discussing the Social Studies: Character - Determination and Accomplishments lesson, help your student set their own goal or two using the space below. Then brainstorm small steps they can take to help them accomplish their goals.

Goal #1 _____

Step 1 _____

Step 2 _____

Step 3 _____

Goal #2 _____

Step 1 _____

Step 2 _____

Step 3 _____

*Tip: Sometimes (if applicable) putting a picture with their written goal might help keep them focused on the "prize."

Little Nino's Pizzeria

Title:	*Little Nino's Pizzeria*
Author:	Karen Barbour
Illustrator:	Karen Barbour
Copyright:	1987
Summary:	Nino and his son Tony discover that bigger is not always better.

Social Studies: Relationship - Father & Son

Tony and his father have a good relationship. They work together making pizza. They serve together. They clean up together. They even give together, to people who have no food. His dad's smiles and arm around the shoulder show Tony that he is important and appreciated.

Then there comes a time when Tony's dad is preoccupied. In his new job he has so many new things to do that he forgets Tony. Tony doesn't throw a tantrum or get bitter, but he does withdraw and you can see the sadness on his face.

At the end of the story Nino decides to return to the things of the past that are important to him. Discuss with your student the fact that relationships, whether with parents, siblings, teachers, friends or others are not always exactly the same. Tony's dad didn't stop loving him. But he is distracted for awhile. Tony could react differently, and become bitter or feel rejected. Talk about the fact that distractions and misunderstandings often affect relationships, but keeping a loving heart and having patience often result in happy endings.

Do you think it is possible that the pizzeria is named Little Nino's (even though Nino is quite big) because his dad named it for him when he was young? Later,

Nino renames the restaurant "Little Tony's" in honor of his son.

This story takes place in a busy, modern city. Place your story disk on a city that you and your student think might serve "the best pizza in the world"!

Social Studies: Good Communication

One of the most important human relationship skills is to communicate well with others in a friendly, honest way, avoiding if possible, harsh, angry words and arguments. There is a good example of this kind of communication between Tony's dad and the man in the green suit. The "money man" makes a proposal to Nino and he agrees to certain things. (Nino would manage the new restaurant and he would get paid very well.) When Tony's dad discovers he does not enjoy the new job, he talks with the restaurant owner. The picture of them shaking hands shows that the communication was cordial and ends on a friendly basis. This good communication allows both men to continue their own work without the burden of bad feelings. It may not always work like this, but there should always be an attempt to communicate on a friendly and respectful basis.

If appropriate, discuss with your student some basic good communication skills, including avoiding the antagonistic "you always" or "you never" statements, name calling and arguing. Learning to listen respectfully and carefully is also an important part of good communication.

Social Studies: Family Business

Tony's dad makes the best pizza. What are the text and picture clues to the fact that his pizzeria is a family business? (Tony's mother and baby brother or sis-ter are around as he and his dad make pizza. Tony is young but he gets to help a great deal. Nino makes the decision to close the pizzeria and open another restaurant, and later makes the decision to re-open the pizzeria and change the name. These are all things he can do if he runs his own business.)

In FIAR Vol. 1, *Night of the Moonjellies*, by Mark Shasha, you read about a boy who helps in a family-run business. Compare the boys and their jobs in the stories, if you wish.

Some of the duties involved in running a small business are: purchasing supplies, paying bills (i.e., electricity, water, hired help, building payments, supply costs, insurance), possibly cooking, cleaning, waiting on customers, paying quarterly and monthly taxes, etc. Ask your student if he thinks he would enjoy running a small family business and if so, what kind? There is some additional information on the topic of family business in the lessons for *Night of the Moonjellies*, by Mark Shasha (FIAR Vol. 1) and in *Mirette on the Highwire*, by Emily Arnold McCully (FIAR Vol. 2).

Social Studies: Character - Servant Heart

Through the FIAR books Vol. 1 and 2, you have seen some people with special character traits. The characters in these stories do not possess all the same traits. Each one has different strengths. In *Little Nina's Pizzeria*, Tony has a remarkable gift of serving. He enjoys it. **Serving and helping** is what makes him happy. Just look at his face when he has no place to help. Tony enjoys helping his dad make pizza and he loves to serve the people their meals. He is proud of the pizza he and his dad make and is happy to wait on the customers. He even knows how to pick up the plates and carry out the dirty dishes! In doing these things, he is happy. (Remember Mirette, FIAR Vol.

2, *Mirette on the Highwire*, who helps run the boardinghouse? She knows how to do things well and she cheerfully helps, but Tony seems to thrive on it!)

Tony is rewarded for his faithfulness and desire to help when his father reopens the pizzeria and names it "Little Tony's", in honor of his son. The next to the last picture shows Tony with an addition to his uniform—a chef's hat! (Watch for chefs' hats on cooking shows and point them out to your student. Teachers, just for your information: These tall white hats are called *toque blanche* in France which means "white hat." They often have pleats around the headband, sometimes as many as a hundred, to represent how many ways a chef knows to fix an egg! Some soufflé dishes look like these hats.)

Everyone can learn to serve cheerfully when the need arises, but to Tony it is a constant way of life. With your student, discuss people that you've met who may have been like Tony. Does he know any people like that? (Again, everyone does not have the same strengths, and the differences in good character traits among people gives the pleasing variety of life.)

Social Studies: The Homeless

Little Nino and Tony served pizzas to the "hungry people in the alley who had no homes." This story provides a chance to introduce the subject of the homeless if you desire, and to mention compassion as another character trait shared by Tony and his father.

Notice the homeless people. When do they show up again in the story? (They are on the street, looking on as Tony walks home dejected. They are there when Little Tony's opens, and in the last picture, as well as on the back cover.)

Language Arts: Theme

Ask your student what he thinks is the main idea of the story. This main idea is called a theme. A theme is often stated as a phrase, and in the case of *Little Nino's Pizzeria*, one might say: "Bigger isn't always better," or maybe "Money isn't everything," or "Better a little with contentment." A sub-theme might be, "Find the work that you were meant to do; it will make you happy." When you discuss the main idea of a story with young children it lays the foundation for exploring themes they will someday find in more complicated works of literature. As you talk about the themes or main ideas in this story include some of the following topics: Nino accepts the manager's job and tries a new career. But, in this particular case, he finds that bigger is not always better. His duties are more managerial and far less creative. He isn't used to that. He probably misses working with his son and having his family around him, as well as cooking the pizza. The wonderful thing about Nino is that he has the courage to give up the extra money and return to the work that makes him happy. It means a lot to Tony, too!

Language Arts: Homophones

Does your older student remember homophones? Remind him of *Truman's Aunt Farm*. Now can he remember? Ant and Aunt? Homophones are words that sound alike, but are not spelled alike, and they have different meanings. In *Little Nino's Pizzeria*, Tony says he helps knead the dough. This word (write it on a vocabulary card and draw hands working bread dough) "knead" means to fold bread dough over and over to help make the rising process more successful. Ask your student what word it sounds like. ("need:" as in, "I need help with my reading.") It may bring a smile to your student to figure out a sentence that uses both words. For example: "We *need* a person to *knead* the dough," or "there's no *need* to *knead* that dough any longer."

Art: Full-Color Palette and Medium

Did your student enjoy the bright color illustrations? Karen Barbour used **gouache** (gwash—rhymes with squash) and watercolors for her pictures. You can see the effects of both media on the back cover illustration. At the top, above the buildings, are some areas where the paint shows white paper through, like watercolor. But most of the rest of the picture is made of opaque solid colors. Another example is the picture where Tony feeds pizza to the people in the alley who have no homes. Again, the sky shows some translucence, but compare this look to the opaque, solid color of Tony's pants. Also, look under Tony's feet for the "watercolor wash" look, and compare to the (gouache) solid yellow of the dog. (Gouache is paint pigment, mixed with water and gum, which makes this medium a watercolor type paint but it is opaque. This means you can't see through to paper. Ordinary watercolor, which is translucent, allows the paper to show through the paints.)

Warm weather provides a wonderful opportunity to experiment with **watercolor** paints and try new subjects, even outdoor subjects. Use a clipboard and take your paints outside. Find an old tree. Draw it first lightly with pencil, notice any shadows, type of bark, etc. Then use watercolors to finish the work. Or capture in drawing the repetition of the top of a wooden fence, or anything that is interesting and has simple design, like an old flower pot. Then paint in the color. When using the paints, remember to let areas dry (play a game between colors) before going to the next color. In some instances, like the sky, you may want some color running together. And remember to clean your brush well with water between colors. Most of all, have fun!

Art: Comparing Artist to Artist

The illustrations of *Little Nino's Pizzeria* are reminiscent of some of the work of the French artist Henri Matisse (ma-TEES). Look in the juvenile section of your library for a book introducing Matisse that is written for children. (Preview it anyway!) See if the painting titled "Harmony in Red" is included in the book's picture plates. This picture shows bright colors. The woman figure in the picture is flat (no rounding, or shading) and she is seen in profile like many of the illustrations in *Little Nino's Pizzeria*. Among other famous works of Matisse that children might enjoy are: "Goldfish," "Interior with Violin," "Still Life with a Magnolia," etc.

Art: Symbolism

Look with your student at the illustration when the man comes to see Tony's dad after the last pizza. What does the man want from Tony's dad? (He wants him to close Little Nino's Pizzeria and manage a large new restaurant.) What does he tell the father the result will be? (More money) Now, have your student look carefully at the man in the green suit. What mark is patterned over the suit? ($$$) This is a symbol for money. Look at his cuff links. (More $$ signs. Look out the door at his expensive limousine. Explain the word limousine, if necessary, and mention this is a type of car generally used by wealthy people.) The artist uses the money signs to symbolize that, in a popular **idiom**, this man is "made of money;" that is, he has a lot of money. (**Teacher's Note:** Young children are often confused by popular **idioms**. Phrases like "give in" which means to yield, or "the food's on the house," which means that someone else is paying for it, are often taken literally by the young. That is why the idiom "made of money" is referenced here, to introduce them to the saying and what it actually means. Remember that the conversations of adults can often be misunderstood if they are not explained. Have fun identifying idioms as you come across them during the year.)

Look at the title page. With your student notice the "money man," eating pizza. Next, from the beginning of the story, look through the pictures. Let your student discover the first time the wealthy money man appears in the story. (He is sitting at Little Nino's eating a pizza, p. 7.) When is the next time you see him? (Standing in the long lines because Little Nino's is so popular, p. 10.) Ask your student why he thinks the money man asks Tony's dad to come and manage his new restaurant. (Perhaps because he has observed, at least twice, the father working hard making an extremely successful business.)

Art: Illustrations-Action, Emotion and Personification

Watch the expressions on the faces of Tony, his mother and his dad in the pictures of the story. Their faces tell a lot about what they are feeling. But even more expressive than their faces is their body posture. Follow Tony as he joyfully helps make and serve pizza. Then notice the protective arm around his father as the man in the green suit makes his proposal. Watch Tony as he finds there is no place for him in the restaurant and the total dejection that stoops his shoulders as he walks home. Quickly turn the page and see the same stooped shoulders on his father, and the same "head in hands"-type sadness on both their faces. This is such a contrast from their extremely straight and tall postures and the smiling expressions of earlier pictures!

The mother has a protective arm around the father now, as he explains his problem. And last, enjoy the celebration and animation as Nino decides to do what he loves. Once again, Tony finds his "helper's" place along side his father. Nino ends this exchange with his arm around both his wife and Tony.

From the beginning, follow the expressions on the faces of the dog and cat throughout the story. Look, too, at their bodies. Ask your student to point out when they look happy, worried, sad or content.

Also look at the moon. Does the expression on the face of the moon remain constant, or does it change? (The expression on the face of the moon does change. Name these expressions, such as smiling, watchful, sad, laughing, ecstatic. The illustrator uses **personification** to give these human expressions and emotions to the face of the moon.)

Have your enthusiastic art student try a short story that shows his characters in a wide range of emotions. The plot should develop to show the reasons for these emotions. Let him illustrate the story (even put it into book format). He could even include a minor non-human character or inanimate object personified to reflect the emotions of the story as the cat, dog and moon do in *Little Nino's Pizzeria*. For instance a tree (personified with a face) can look on, in your student's story, and be happy or scared or puzzled or sad, as the action happens with the human characters. In the same way, a bowl of fruit on the table, with an apple in it personified can reflect the emotions of the story. The face of a grandfather clock, or almost any animal or object can be used.

Your older student can have fun learning to imitate personification which artists often use in children's illustrations. Or, you make up a story with personification that your younger student can illustrate.

Art: Details That Enhance the Text

Often, one gains additional information about the story from the pictures. Things not directly mentioned in the text are picked up by careful observation of the illustrations. In *Little Nino's Pizzeria*, one of the interesting details revealed by the pictures are the occupations of the people who come to eat pizza. Their shirts give clues to the kinds of job they have. Let your reading student look at the illustrations and try to find some for himself. Point out to your younger student the different shirts, i.e., "Look! That man eating pizza must sell people tires for their cars and repair flats." (Your student may reply, "How do you know?") Then you can respond, "Because the back of his shirt says Jack's Tire Shop." Other occupational clues are: Joe's Rug Shop, Pier 23, etc.

Also, there are **families** who come to eat at Little Nino's and again later when the name is changed to Little Tony's. However, there are no children pictured in the fancy restaurant. So, even though it is never mentioned in the text, the detailed pictures show that Nino has changed more than just a building and duties, but his clientele as well.

Math: Counting and Measurements of Weight

Your younger student can count the pepperonis and other toppings on the pizzas, or the money signs on the man's green suit.

With your older student, you might look at the first

four pictures of the story and discuss how each of the ingredients are weighed for purchase. For instance: tomatoes, peppers and onions are purchased by the pound and weighed on a produce scale. Flour usually comes in 5, 10, 25, 50, or 100-pound sacks. Olive oil is purchased in a bottle, with liquid ounce measurements, or a large can or even barrels, and is measured with liquid measurements, like quarts or gallons. Cheese usually comes by ounces or pounds. Spices like salt, pepper, oregano, and basil come in small containers by the ounce or in large bulk amounts weighed in pounds.

Science: Foods and Food Groups

Pizza can have a surprising number of ingredients. Make a list of all the foods that Nino and Tony used to make their pizza (tomatoes, onions, green peppers, garlic, mushrooms, flour, olive oil, cheeses, pepperoni, sausage, spices—basil, oregano, salt and pepper.) A colorful list could be made by printing the name of each ingredient, drawing beside it a picture of the item and coloring it brightly with colors like the story! Allow your student to include pizza toppings that might be familiar to him that were not included in Nino's pizza. Perhaps olives, Canadian bacon, pineapple, anchovies, sun-dried tomatoes, pesto or spinach!

Have your older student classify the pizza ingredients into food groups, in order to determine if pizza has a balance of nutrients:

Milk and Milk Products	Cheeses
Meats	Pepperoni and Sausage, Anchovies
Breads and Cereals	Flour
Fruits and Vegetables	Tomatoes, Green Peppers, Onion, Garlic, Olives, Spinach, Mushrooms, Pineapple

Now ask your student if pizza has a balance of good nutrients. (If the fats are held to a moderate amount, pizza can be a well balanced meal.)

Science: Cooking

Cooking pizza involves watching a plant grow (**yeast**), making sauce (**mixture**), using food from plants and animals, using a **heat source** and creating food that has **calories**.

But most of all, making pizza is fun! So throw a pizza party and invite your student's friends. If you are making pizza from scratch, then each friend can be assigned a pizza ingredient to bring. Make the pizza, or help them make it, decorate and bake it. Take photographs of the pizza-making process and add them to your student's notebook.

Then, read them this story while you are waiting for the pizza to cook!

Teacher's Notes

The *Five in a Row* lesson options for each unit in the manual are all you need to teach your child. The additional resource area provided below is simply a place to jot down relevant info you've found that you might want to reference.

LITTLE NINO'S PIZZERIA

Date: _____

Student: _____

Five in a Row Lesson Topics Chosen:

Social Studies:
_____
_____
_____

Language Arts:
_____
_____
_____

Art:
_____
_____
_____

Math:
_____
_____
_____

Science:
_____
_____
_____

Relevant Library Resources:
Books, DVDs, Audio Books
_____
_____
_____
_____
_____
_____

Websites or Video Links:
_____
_____
_____
_____
_____
_____
_____
_____
_____

194

Related Field Trip Opportunities:
_____
_____
_____

Favorite Quote or Memory During Study:
_____
_____
_____

Name:

Date:

Social Studies: **Family Business**

Your student might find it fun to pretend he runs a Pizzeria. He can create the menu (with prices!) and take your order on the guest check below.

Sample Menu

Pizza

	Slice	Pie
Cheese	$1	$8
Pepperoni	$3	$16
Vegetable	$2	$12

Drinks

Soda	$2
Tea	$1
Water	$0

Desserts

Pie	$2
Cake	$2
Candy	$1

Restaurant: _____

Guest Check

SERVER	TABLE	GUESTS	CHECK NUMBER

	TAX	
Thank You	TOTAL	

After reading and classifying the pizza ingredients build a healthy, well-balanced pizza by circling ingredient names on the pizza below.

196

Green Bell Pepper

Pepperoni

Sausage

Pineapple

Bacon

Beef

Black Olives

Onion

Cheese

Meatballs

Mushrooms

Canadian Bacon

Spinach

Grilled Chicken

Tomatoes

Anchovies

Name:

Date:

Social Studies: **Opportunities to Serve**

To dive deeper into the Social Studies: Character - Servant Heart lesson you can use this activity sheet to discuss opportunities that your student might have to serve family, friends or their community.

Make a list together of ways your student (or family) might serve others.

Serve Family	Serve Friends	Serve Community
_____	_____	_____
_____	_____	_____
_____	_____	_____
_____	_____	_____
_____	_____	_____
_____	_____	_____
_____	_____	_____
_____	_____	_____
_____	_____	_____

*Community could include neighbors, church, small businesses, doctors or dentist offices, mail carrier, grocery store, police and firefighters, etc.

The Old Woman Who Named Things

Title: *The Old Woman Who Named Things*
Author: Cynthia Rylant
Illustrator: Kathryn Brown
Copyright: 1996
Summary: A stray puppy teaches an old woman an important lesson about love and its benefits.

Social Studies: Naming Inanimate Objects

Has your family ever named your car or your house as the old woman did in Cynthia Rylant's story? Naming cars, boats or houses with people's names is fairly common. But any inanimate thing can also be named. The western hero Davy Crockett, who fought at the Alamo, had a rifle given to him that he named "Old Betsy." Mike Mulligan named his steam shovel Mary Anne (FIAR Vol. 1). If your student has interest, have her find an inanimate "something special" to name. She could always have a favorite tree named George, or a bird bath named Christine—the possibilities are limitless!

Social Studies: Character - Compassion and Kindness

The old woman noticed the stray puppy was hungry. She did not want a puppy, so she had a decision to make. She could have ignored him, or she could have thrown a stick at him and chased him away. But she felt a compassion for him and went to find him something to eat.

People always have the choice to make to either be kind to the animals that enter their lives or to be cruel. Has your student ever seen someone kick at a dog or cat?

It is always better to be kind to animals, but of course that doesn't mean you have to bring all them home or even feed them. Becoming a person given to kindness is much better than ever being cruel.

Make a poster about being kind to animals. What are different ways, big and small, that people can show kindness to all creatures? This can range from moving a stranded worm from the hot sidewalk to the grass, to adopting a homeless pet from a shelter—and everything in between!

Social Studies: Pinpointing History Through Objects

By observing illustrations such as cars and household items, you can often estimate approximate times of stories. If you and your student have read other FIAR books, you probably have experience with this. (*Blueberries for Sal*, Before FIAR; *Lentil*, FIAR Vol. 1; *When I Was Young in the Mountains*, FIAR Vol. 2, for example.) This story appears to take place in the 1950s or later. How do we know? Look at the car and truck depicted in this story. They are not like the cars of today, but not quite as old as the cars in some other FIAR books your student has studied. You could call these "mid-century automobiles" because they look to be the type driven during the middle of the 20th century.

Of course, just because the car is old doesn't mean the story necessarily takes place during that time. Some people today have antique cars. So what is another important clue in the illustrations as to the possible time of the story? With your student, look at the phone that sits on the small table in the old woman's house. This type of phone would have been used by many people during the same time that the car was driven.

Looking for clues to help date stories can be fun. In the illustrations and sometimes the text, look for clues such as clothing, types of vehicles, and items of communication and media such as telephones, televisions, computers, etc. Dating the events of a story can be a veritable detective hunt. Learning to search for such clues increases your student's powers of observation and knowledge of history.

Social Studies: Geography Guesses

Just as your student made observations in order to pinpoint *when* this story takes place, there is also an opportunity to guess *where* it might take place. The location of this book isn't mentioned, but there are some clues that might help your student decide where to put the story disk.

If your student is older, she may find clues on her own, based on the illustrations. With a younger student, go through each page and look for things that could indicate where the story takes place. Some ideas might be:

- The old woman wears western (cowboy) boots.
- Biscuits, ham and cheese are foods often favored in southern states.
- There are many flowers in the illustrations.
- The old woman does have on sweater, so it isn't always hot.
- There is rain where she lives; people have umbrellas and there is mud on Betsy's fender and rusty hinges on the gate.

You can place your story disk on your spot for a make-believe place, or declare a state based on all the clues that are listed here and that your student can add, and put it there (Texas, perhaps?). Have your student give her reasons why she chose the place that she did. Perhaps if you have more than one student they may choose different places for different reasons. This is an exercise in wondering and thinking through clues and making a choice. Since there is no right or wrong to this exercise, different decisions could be interesting!

Language Arts: Name the Character

After reading this book, did you or your student ever want to name the old woman? She names things all throughout the book, but she doesn't have one herself! Would your student like to give her a name? It could be something floral because she likes flowers and there are so many in the illustrations. What about a name like "Lily Gardner?" Or "Charity Hart," because charity is an older word for love and kindness. Or "Bea" for her beehive hairdo? Of course, there is no right or wrong answer. Ask your student what she thinks would be a perfect name for this kind and wonderful lady.

Language Arts: Climax and Denouement

In previous FIAR volumes, your student may have learned about the elements of a story: conflict, rising action, climax, and denouement (day new MAHN). The climax of a story is the highest or most exciting point of the plot and action. In this story the excitement is building as the woman misses the dog visiting her and is trying to come to terms with what to do about that.

When a simple phone call to the dog pound does not get the result she desires, it becomes decision time for the old woman. There is excitement building (I will go find the dog), which she then begins to refer to as "my dog." As the dogcatcher asks the old woman for the name of "her dog" the climax is reached!

"My dog's *name* is Lucky." The old woman cares more for the dog than her fears and names him!

The denouement is the final resolution and outcome of the story. This occurs after the climax point as the story ends with the details of the happy dog and the happy woman. For a younger student, it isn't important that you teach the word denouement, but rather that you might mention the idea of a story's climax (highest, most exciting part) and then that there are a few details left after that—the "coming down" from the high point to the conclusion of the story. If you mention this casually, your student will begin to understand this idea, and as you continue to study stories you can remind her of these concepts as a review.

Language Arts: Personification

The inanimate (non-living) things that cannot die as a living creature could, are cheerfully named by the old woman. She names and gives some human characteristics to her car, chair, house and more. These all are personified by naming them. If you have used Five in a Row for a while, can your student name other FIAR stories that have used personification? *Mike Mulligan and His Steam Shovel, Ping, Katy and the Big Snow, The Little Red Lighthouse and the Great Gray Bridge*, and others. See the Art lesson later in this unit for more details on personification.

Art: Details - Discovering the Little Things

Look through Kathryn Brown's illustrations and notice how many different outfits the old woman is wearing. Does she wear each outfit more than once throughout the days of the story? These are tiny details. They are not critical to the love of the story, but mentioning them lightly in fun does increase observational skills. Here are more small details to point out and enjoy with your student:

In the picture where we first see the old woman getting into bed, look at her socks. This is a type of sock which would be warm and durable under cowboy boots. This sock with the red heel was originally manufactured as work socks by a company in Illinois around 1890. The socks, with their famous seamless heel, became known as "Rockford Red Heels" by the early 1930s, During the Great Depression, people first began to make "sock monkeys" out of the worn-out socks. Look online for images of a sock monkey, which is still popular even today.

Check back through the story and discover the old woman's pictures if you didn't notice them at first. What kinds of pictures does she have in her house? What might that tell you about her, where she lives, or what is important to her?

Why does the dog sit at the pound gate rather than run around with the other dogs? (He was noticing Betsy, the car.)

What is the topic of the book the old woman is reading? (everlasting flowers) There really is a flower that is called an everlasting flower (also called strawflower), and after all, with the old woman's fears of those she loved dying, what other flower would she be reading about? (This may be humorous to the teacher only!)

The old woman visited the dogcatcher's kennel and looked for her dog. When did the dog come to her? He came to her voice, as she called out his name.

Did your student notice the different dressers in the illustrations? The text of the story does say that she got a new dresser and named it Bill, but did your student notice the difference in the old dresser and the new one? Noticing is a bit more difficult here because the text of the story about the change was not on either page with the illustrations of the dressers. See if your student notices this on her own, or provide small clues to help her discover it herself. Or, simply point it out and observe how the author and illustrator must work together to make the whole story unified and fun to read.

Art: Illustrations - Watercolor Palette

Kathryn Brown used watercolors in her illustrations for *The Old Woman Who Named Things*. Her paintings have a gentle, whimsical feel to them, which also describes the old woman, don't you think? The text and the illustrations go well together.

The palette (the range of colors used) follows throughout the story with lots of pastel colors such as aqua and peach, and even the brighter reds are more of a warm red with yellow, rather than a cooler red with blue.

Art: Patterns - Paisley

The old woman's blue pants on the cover of the book have yellow paisley patterns on them. Paisley is a pattern of teardrop-shaped designs originating in Persia hundreds of years ago. Although this pattern has been popular in many cultures for centuries, paisley had a resurgence in the United States in the 1960s on clothing and other articles (napkins, tablecloths, curtains, sheets, wallpaper, etc.). Are there any paisley items in your student's home (perhaps on a necktie, scarf, etc.)? Search for paisley images online and notice the wide range of colors and patterns. Your student may want to reproduce a paisley pattern in her favorite colors using paints, crayons, or colored pencils, or make up her own.

Art: Perspective

The chair (Fred) is a large piece of furniture. But in the picture where we see the old woman from the outside through her front window—when she is sad that the dog has quit coming to see her—she looks so sad and so small. Isn't that a great use of illustration to show how she was feeling small and forlorn? Also, this illustration looks a bit like the little old woman is in a small box—as if she is locked up in a box of worry and fear.

A good illustrator must not only *read* the story she will do the artwork for, but she needs to be able to *feel* the emotions of the characters and portray those emotions and actions as well. Just as an actor tries to imagine the emotions of the character she is playing, and tries to "live" in her role, a good illustrator will try to "live" in the story so that her artwork enhances the text. It's good to discuss this with your student if she enjoys writing stories and illustrating her own work.

Your student may want to try a drawing that uses perspective in this way. By picturing something very large alongside something small, what emotion or feeling will your student portray? Sadness, strength, fear, worry, confidence, awe, uncertainty—any could be possible, depending on the subject of the drawing, facial expressions, etc.

Art: Personification

The chair, car, house and bed were some of the things the old woman named in the story. On each of these you can see two eyes and a mouth—they were personified both by text *and* by illustration.

If your student has chosen an inanimate thing to name from the lesson in Social Studies: Naming Inanimate Objects, have her draw a picture of her object and see if she can make subtle eyes and nose or mouth to give the impression of a face. If she hasn't chosen an object, she can choose something now from objects around her or from her imagination to personify with facial features. If you still have access to the previous FIAR titles that were mentioned in the Language Arts: Personification lesson, take a look through those books for examples of how different artists show facial features on boats, lighthouses, steam shovels, etc.

Art: Rain

In the illustration showing the old woman in her rain hat driving around town hunting for her visitor-dog, the artist has depicted rain. How does your student like to illustrate rain?

For another look at how an artist portrays rain, search online for images by Takahashi Shotei-Hiroaki of a rainy day in Japan. You'll find many images by this 20th century woodblock artist, painter, and printmaker. Compare the various ways he portrayed rain in his illustrations.

Math: Days, Months, Years

"This went on for many months. The puppy got bigger and bigger until soon it wasn't a puppy anymore. It was a dog." How long does it take a puppy to grow to adulthood? First there is the pregnancy (gestation) time when the puppy is growing in its mother. The gestation period for dogs is generally between 58 and 68 days (compare that to human gestation of 9 months, or about 270 days). Dogs are full grown between 10 and 18 months, depending on breed, with the smaller breeds maturing more quickly. Lucky is a medium-sized dog, so he would be full grown at about a year.

Your student will probably find it interesting that different animals have greatly different gestation periods. Opossums, hamsters and rabbits have very short gestation periods, while elephants, giraffes and whales have some of the longest. Hippos, gorillas, and cows have gestation periods similar to humans. Explore with your student how many days, months or years certain animals are pregnant or how old they are when fully grown.

Science: Dogs and Breeds

This is your chance to study as much or as little as you wish about dogs, breeds, training, grooming, etc. This field of study is vast! Fortunately, your student can find an abundance of information online and in the library, both on dogs in general and on specific breeds.

You may have already touched on the science topic of classification, either just in passing or in depth. In the animal kingdom (kingdom **Animalia**), the first division asks whether or not the animal has a backbone. Those without a backbone are called **invertebrates** and those with a backbone are called **vertebrates**. Dogs would be classified in which category? Vertebrates, because dogs have backbones. Then there are five groups of animals with backbones, each of which is a class. The dog is in the class **Mammalia** (mammals). If your student is interested in the further classification, the order is **Carnivora** (meat eater), the family is **Canidae** (dog family), and the genus and species is **Canis familiaris**. Is your student familiar with the word canine or has she seen a "K-9" police vehicle? Point out the similarity between the words Canis and canine. She might also find the species name fun and interesting: familiaris … doesn't that sound a lot like "familiar" or "family"? Ask her why she thinks that is the species name for a dog.

(**Teacher's information:** The American Kennel Club recognizes over 200 breeds of dog! If your family would like to get a puppy or dog in the future, you can find dog breed selector quizzes online to help you decide which dog might be best for you. These quizzes can also be a fun learning activity to acquire information about specific breeds.)

Additional activities for this topic might include: finding a favorite breed and learning more about it, visiting a vet's office or kennel, doing a project to raise money for an animal shelter, or visiting a pet store.

Science: Birds

On the dedication page of the story there is an Eastern bluebird. This bird, a type of thrush, measures 6 to 8 inches long and is found in woodlands, orchards, and farmlands. Bluebirds eat beetles, crickets, grasshoppers and caterpillars, and if insects are not available, they will eat berries or seeds. Your student may enjoy drawing this beautiful bird and listing some interesting facts about it. Other activities could be to research favorite birds, birds in your own area, your state bird, migration patterns, nests of different birds, eggs of different birds, flightless birds, etc.

Did your student notice two more birds later in the book? (They are perched on the old woman's new concrete pig statue in her garden.)

(**Teacher's Note:** Refer to the Science: Dogs and Breeds lesson for further information on animal classification.) Birds are vertebrates (because they have backbones) belonging to the scientific class Aves. Birds are different in many ways, but have these things in common: they are warm-blooded, they have feathers (although not all fly), they lay eggs, and they have a strong, lightweight skeleton.

Teacher's Notes

The *Five in a Row* lesson options for each unit in the manual are all you need to teach your child. The additional resource area provided below is simply a place to jot down relevant info you've found that you might want to reference.

THE OLD WOMAN WHO NAMED THINGS

Date:

Student:

206

Five in a Row Lesson Topics Chosen:

Social Studies:

Language Arts:

Art:

Math:

Science:

**Relevant Library Resources:
Books, DVDs, Audio Books**

Websites or Video Links:

Related Field Trip Opportunities:

Favorite Quote or Memory During Study:

Name:

Date:

Science: **Dog Breeds**

Choose two distinctly different breeds of dogs. Print and paste their pictures into the frames below. Research the two breeds and write some of their characteristics below their pictures.

Breed: _____   Breed: _____

Characteristics: Characteristics:

_____   _____

_____   _____

_____   _____

_____   _____

_____   _____

_____   _____

_____   _____

Characteristics might include: *Size, Energy, Job, Personality, Behavior, Grooming,* etc.

The gestation period (when a puppy is growing in its mother) for a dog is generally between 58 and 68 days.

Question 1.

About how many months is a typical dog's gestation?
Remember, there are 28-31 days in a month.

Answer _____

Question 2.

Typically a puppy can go home to its new owner at 8 weeks. How many months old would that puppy be?
On average, there are 4 weeks in a month.

Answer _____

Question 3. (for your older student)

The average lifespan for a dog is 10-13 years. How many months old would a dog be if it reached 13 years?

Answer _____

Name:

Date:

Science: **Animal Gestation**

Choose another animal to study and compare its gestation to that of a dog. Print and paste pictures of a dog and the second animal you choose into the frames below. Write in the information that you learn about each next to their picture.

Animal: <u>DOG</u>

Gestation in Days _____

or Months _____

Full-Grown at _____

Animal: _____

Gestation in Days _____

or Months _____

Full-Grown at _____

Review Week

If you'd like, take a week to review the books, authors and illustrators you've studied in *Five in a Row* Vol. 3. Recall which titles were award-winners and figure out which book is the oldest, and which book was written the most recently. Discuss the stories you and your student particularly liked and which characters or ideas were your favorites. Gather all the story disks for Volume 3 and see if your student can name each one. Let her put them in order beginning with her favorite, next favorite, etc.

Look again at the artwork in any books you still have. Review the elements of art that you have learned. If you have kept an illustrated chart of art definitions and elements, review it now. Look at the artwork your student has done during these lessons and point out examples you feel are outstanding. Let her see how much she has learned. Use specific compliments such as "Your use of line and design is excellent in this picture," "I enjoy the variety of colors you chose for this work," "This picture is so full of expression and action, I almost want to jump right in!" or "The balance is pleasing in this scene."

If your student has kept a notebook, leaf through it with her. Recall various projects and review concepts in Social Studies (Traditions, Culture, Transition to Industrial Age, Shyness, Loneliness, Paul Revere's Ride, etc.), Geography (Kansas, the Yukon, Maine, Ohio, Mountains, etc.), Science (Ants, Salamanders, Sheep, Wheat, Bees, Fog, Altitude, etc.) and Math (Measuring, Tallying.)

Review the vocabulary words by using your illustrated list or illustrated file box. Recall the stories in which they appear and practice using the words in sentences.

See how many story disks your student can correctly place on the U.S. or world map. If you have studied and made disks for mountain ranges, rivers or Great Lakes, etc., practice placing those on the map, too. Remember to practice directions, and compass points on the map, around the classroom, and on outings.

Thank you for using *Five in a Row*. I hope you had a wonderful time learning together with stories that you'll remember. If you've enjoyed *Five in a Row* Vol. 3, please share it with a friend!

Five in a Row Volume Three Story Disks

Sample **Lesson Planning Sheet**

Sample Lesson Planning Page: *The Duchess Bakes a Cake* has 19 suggested lessons in the lesson portion of this manual. The sample planning sheet above shows 8 ideas that *could* be chosen for a one-week study. You are free to choose *any* of the 19 lesson ideas and keep track of your choices by noting them on the reproducible, blank Lesson Planning Sheet (following page). For more ideas on making the best use of your *Five in a Row* curriculum, be sure to read the *How to Use Five in a Row* section beginning on p. 10.

	Monday	Tuesday
Title: *The Duchess Bakes a Cake*	**Social Studies** Read story through, then: Dicsuss Middle Ages 1. Kings- Kingdoms 2. Dukes- Duchess 3. Knights 4. Castles 5. Feudal system	**Language Arts** Read story through, then: Do the story as a play!
Author: Virgina Kahl		
Illustrator: Virgina Kahl		

Wednesday	Thursday	Friday
Art	**Math**	**Science**
Read story through, then:	Read story through, then:	Read story through, then:
Action Figure Tracings	The Number 13 Talk about superstitions.	Bake a cake! Talk about calories.
Make a castle out of cardboard boxes	Some people think 13 is unlucky. Many buildings don't have a 13th floor.	Make a list of good, healthy snacks and desserts to have on a regular basis.
Read some from "King Arthur" or "The Door in the Wall" by de Angeli	Others find 13 a bonus ... like a baker's dozen!	

Lesson Planning Sheet

	Monday	Tuesday
Title:		
Author:		
Illustrator:		
Award:		

Wednesday	Thursday	Friday

Choices a Writer Can Make

Choices an Artist Can Make

Finding the Books

Much has changed in the library system, due to internet access, since *Five in a Row* was first published. Some of the book titles in Volumes 1-3 may be out of print, and your local library branch may not own all the titles that are in print. However, it is easier than ever to search your library's online catalogue and request/hold titles. Even Interlibrary Loan (ILL) is something you can search from your home computer, through your library's website.

Not all library systems are exactly alike, but most online searches work in a similar way. You will sign in to your library system online with your library card number. Your personal account will show books you've requested or placed on hold and books you've checked out. Some systems even have virtual bookshelves where you can place titles for the future or that you've completed. If your online library system has this, it would be convenient to place the FIAR titles on your "future shelf" so that you can quickly go there to request a title or two for your upcoming studies.

When searching your library system's catalogue or the ILL catalogue, here are a few tips. Sometimes a book title won't be found when you search for it. Before giving up or moving on to ILL, try searching the author's name instead. Many times a book can be found listed with all of the author's other books even if it isn't found through a title search. This is true of the ILL catalogue system as well.

Placing several titles on hold every week or two will bring a consistent flow of books cycling in and will allow you to choose which one to use next. By requesting titles online you save yourself the time and effort of searching for books in person. The librarians will locate the book, shelved or misshelved. They will flag the computer to automatically hold the title for you when another library patron returns the book. The ILL requests will automatically happen through the libraries' computer systems. The requested book will be placed on hold for you and shipped to your requested library to be picked up next time you stop by. All of this will save you valuable time and energy!

As your local library collects your requested titles, they will notify you to let you know another book or two is being held for you. What could be easier?

220

If your library does not carry a *Five in a Row* title, or any book, that you wish they had on their shelves, it's a good idea to request it. The reason for this is that a library will sometimes eventually purchase a book if it's requested often enough. So if the library comes up empty-handed on a particular title, keep requesting it every few weeks. Encourage your friends to request it too! You'd be surprised how many wonderful books end up in the system that way. (Your library may have a quick and easy way to do this: check their website to see if they have an option for "Make a purchase request.")

A personal anecdote: A dear friend who began reviewing *Five in a Row* many years ago obtained *Who Owns the Sun?* via ILL. When she returned it, she suggested the librarian consider purchasing a copy for the local library. The busy librarian brushed her aside saying, "I'm sorry, but we've already spent our budget for this year; it's out of the question." Our friend simply opened the book and began reading it aloud to the librarian right at the check-out desk! Before she was halfway through, the librarian was wiping away tears as she listened to the poignant story, and by the time our friend finished reading, the librarian grabbed the book from her saying, "I'm going to take $15 from our office supply budget and order this book immediately!"

Sadly, many of the most wonderful books being written today, as well as marvelous classics like *The Story About Ping*, are being supplanted on limited library shelf space by books of far less merit. The library system is designed to respond to patron usage and requests. They buy and maintain what the most people are reading. One of our more subtle opportunities is to bless our communities with wholesome, solid books by requesting them, sharing them with local librarians, or even donating a copy of a special title from time to time. Our libraries are what we make of them!

One final note on the titles used in *Five in a Row*. We know that some of the books are difficult to locate or currently out of print for those who wish to purchase them. While we struggled with this issue, in the end, we concluded that we wanted to offer the very best of the more than 5,000 children's books we've explored and examined. In the first three volumes of FIAR, we've supplied dozens of complete unit study lesson plans—more than enough for two, three, or more years of schooling.

For those who are willing to leave no stone unturned in their search for every FIAR title, we're sure you'll be blessed and rewarded for your trouble. Some of the more difficult titles to find are some of the richest! And, since publication of the first edition of *Five in a Row*, many previously out-of-print titles have come back into print, most notably from our friends at Purple House Press. So keep on the lookout for hard-to-find titles by trading with friends, having relatives check their libraries, requesting again and again locally, exploring used bookstores and thrift stores, etc. Many parents find that they enjoy the excitement of the search!

In the final analysis, we've tried to give you the very "best of the best" from the more than 5,000 children's books Jane has explored in the hopes that each one will be a present joy and a lifetime friend for both you and your children. God bless you and your children as you set out on the wonderful adventure of learning with *Five in a Row*.

Integrating Additional Curricula with *Five in a Row*

For teaching very young children, you will find *Five in a Row* to be an exciting and complete curriculum. Once you make the decision that your student is ready to begin phonics, reading and mathematics, you will want to supplement your *Five in a Row* curriculum with these additional materials.

There are many wonderful products available to help you teach phonics/reading and mathematics. You will find helpful descriptions of available products online or through recommendations from other homeschool parents. You may also want to make plans to see and review these materials firsthand by planning to attend a homeschool convention or curriculum fair in your area. Most of these events occur between March and July each year.

Once you integrate your new reading/phonics and mathematics curricula with *Five in a Row*, your teaching day may look something like this:

Morning

Math instruction
Five in a Row (read the story aloud and discuss one of the five subject areas)
Lunch (Nap or rest time?)

Afternoon

Phonics/Reading instruction

Or perhaps you'll want to do phonics and mathematics in the morning and save your *Five in a Row* until after lunch as a sort of reward for the morning's work. Other families prefer to do *all* their work in the morning, leaving the afternoon free for other pursuits. Arrange your teaching day in whatever way works best for you and your student. Don't be afraid to change or rearrange your schedule to provide variety, flexibility or to try new schedules until you find what works best for you. There is *no* right or wrong way to do it!

If you would like to create a chart for your schedule, it might look like this:

Monday	Tuesday	Wednesday	Thursday	Friday
Math	Math	Math	Math*	Math
Phonics	Phonics	Phonics	Phonics	Phonics
FIAR Social Studies	FIAR Language Arts	FIAR Art	FIAR Applied Math	FIAR Science

*You may or may not want to omit your math curriculum lesson on Thursday and concentrate on the *Five in a Row* math lesson instead. We believe it's important *not* to skip the *Five in a Row* math lesson however, because it teaches your student how mathematics is applied in life all around her including measuring, telling time, counting money, sewing, building, etc. This lesson time will stimulate math curiosity and encourage your student that real-life math is fun!

Finally, if you are using *Five in a Row* with older students (third grade and up), consider adding brief grammar and spelling lessons. Workbooks containing these lessons are available through curriculum catalogs, teacher's stores, bookstores, online and even at your local Walmart! One series that we've found useful (and there are many) is the *Brighter Child Series*. One book is entitled *English & Grammar*, available for multiple grade levels. These and other simple, affordable booklets can supplement *Five in a Row* for

your older students, supplying the needed sequential learning that's appropriate for language arts.

For Science and Social Studies, you will not need to purchase additional curricula, but you might consider having your older student do additional, self-directed reading and reporting on several of the hundreds of topics you will encounter while doing *Five in a Row*.

By enriching *Five in a Row* using advanced, student-directed research and reporting and by supplementing the curriculum with additional work in mathematics, grammar and spelling, you'll find *Five in a Row* can serve as the educational base for your school-age children all the way through the elementary school years.

Parts of a Flag

Throughout the *Five in a Row* stories, your student will learn about many countries and their flags. This page will help your child learn the parts of a flag.

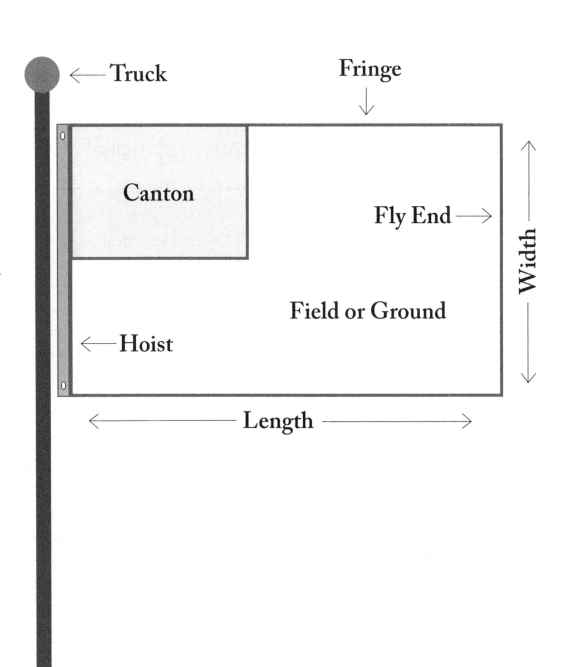

Index

Social Studies

Geography

Language Arts

Taylor, Mark, *Henry the Castaway*, 74

Illustrator Index

Art

Science

Animals - Birds - Insects

Inspired learning through great books.

Five in a Row is a complete,* well-rounded, literature-based curriculum that takes your child from pre-K through middle school.

Current print products available from *Five in a Row* approved retailers:

For ages 2-4:

Before Five in a Row, 2nd Edition – Available from fiveinarow.com and Amazon.com

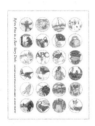

Before Five in a Row Story Disks (full-color, laminated) – Available from fiveinarow.com

Before Five in a Row Storybook Map (full-color, laminated) – Available from fiveinarow.com

For ages 3-5:

More Before Five in a Row – Available from fiveinarow.com and Amazon.com

More Before Five in a Row Story Disks (full-color, laminated) – Available from fiveinarow.com

More Before Five in a Row Storybook Map (full-color, laminated) – Available from fiveinarow.com

For ages 5-9:

Five in a Row Volume 1, Second Edition – Available from fiveinarow.com and Amazon.com

Five in a Row Volume 1 Story Disks (full-color, laminated) – Available from fiveinarow.com

For ages 5-9:

Five in a Row Volume 2, Second Edition – Available from fiveinarow.com and Amazon.com

Five in a Row Volume 2 Story Disks (full-color, laminated) – Available from fiveinarow.com

For ages 5-9:

Five in a Row Volume 3, Second Edition – Available from fiveinarow.com and Amazon.com

Five in a Row Volume 3 Story Disks (full-color, laminated) – Available from fiveinarow.com

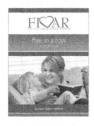

For ages 8 and up:

Five in a Row: Volume 4 (includes Bible Supplement and Cookbook)

Five in a Row Starter Kit: Vols. 1, 2, 3 plus *Five in a Row Bible Supplement*

Five in a Row **Supplements:**

Five in a Row Story Disks (full-color, laminated)

Five in a Row Bible Supplement (for Vols. 1, 2, 3)

Beyond Five in a Row Bible Supplement (for Vols. 1, 2, 3)

Five in a Row Cookbook (for Vols. 1, 2, 3 of both *FIAR* and *Beyond FIAR*)

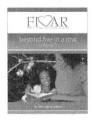

For ages 8-12:
Beyond Five in a Row: Volume 1

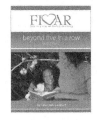

Beyond Five in a Row: Volume 2

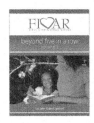

Beyond Five in a Row: Volume 3

For ages 12 and up:
Above & Beyond Five in a Row

Rainbowresource.com currently offers most *Five in a Row* print products as well as Literature Packages that go along with each of the *Five in a Row* and *Beyond Five in a Row* volumes.

Digital resources available from fiveinarow.com

Visit www.fiveinarow.com for additional digital resources and more information on the products above.

FIAR Notebook Builder
More than 120 pages of notebooking templates for all ages, appropriate for any topic or unit of study.

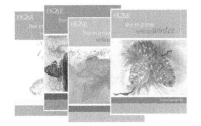

FIAR Nature Studies (Spring, Summer, Fall, Winter)
The *FIAR Nature Study* encourages your entire family to enjoy and explore the outdoors in all four seasons; it is a topic close to Jane's heart. Resources are provided to ensure that you can be a nature mentor to your child! It is a true unit study approach to nature studies; suggestions introduce you and your child to poetry, music, and art that tie in to the season.

FIAR Holiday: Through the Seasons
A treasury of traditions, ideas, and more for making your own special holiday memories.

Homeschool Encouragement Messages (Audio Files)

Inspiring messages from Steve on often-requested topics: Where Do I Begin, I Can't Teach All the Grades at Once, Making Your Children into World Changers, On Becoming Great Teachers, and High School and Beyond.

More digital products available at fiveinarow.com

You'll find other digital products at www.fiveinarow.com, as well, including a *FIAR Planner* and bonus units for Volume 4, as well as other *FIAR* products in digital format: *Above & Beyond FIAR*, the *FIAR Cookbook* and *Holiday* volumes, individual *FIAR Volume 4* units, and *Fold & Learns* for select *FIAR* and *Beyond FIAR* units.

*You will need to add math and phonics/reading instruction to **Five in a Row**.*

Visit fiveinarow.com for additional information on the latest products.